MARRIED BUT FEE

Married but Feeling Alone
Starting Over before It's Too Late

Dr. Greg Cynaumon
and Dana Cynaumon

VINE
BOOKS

Servant Publications
Ann Arbor, Michigan

Vine Books is an imprint of Servant Publications especially designed to serve Evangelical Christians.

The names and characterizations in this book that are drawn from the authors' counseling and personal experiences are rendered pseudonymously and as fictional composites. Any similarity between the names and characters of these individuals and real people is unintended and purely coincidental.

Published by Servant Publications
P.O. Box 8617
Ann Arbor, Michigan 48107

Cover design by A² Graphics

96 97 98 99 10 9 8 7 6 5 4 3

Printed in the United States of America
ISBN 0-89283-902-3

Library of Congress Cataloging-in-Publication Data

Cynaumon, Greg
    Married but feeling alone : starting over before it's too late /
Greg Cynaumon and Dana Cynaumon
        p.   cm.
    ISBN 0-89283-902-3
    1. Marriage.   2. Marriage—Religious aspects—Christianity.
3. Communication in marriage.   4. Married people—Psychology.
5. Loneliness.   6. Intimacy (Psychology)   I. Cynaumon, Dana.
II. Title.
HQ734.C98   1995
248.8'44—dc20   95-24160
                                                        CIP

Dedication

Dedicated with all my love
to Jan, Tracy, and Matthew.
To my parents, Ed and Myrna, thanks for being there!
To my brother Dana for your skillfulness. Thanks!
To Pam for your help and tolerance.

To all marriages in need of a little grace.

Contents

Introduction

I kept glancing at my watch as our pastor bravely ventured into that dangerous territory known as the Sunday lunch hour. I was beginning to understand why Mark Twain once said, "Few sinners are saved after the first twenty minutes of a sermon."

Despite mass fidgeting and a chorus of crying babies, he kept right on preaching.

The topic that morning was active listening... I think. I was too busy thinking about where to take my family to eat after church. Suddenly, I was snapped back to attention with this statement: "The loneliest person tonight isn't sleeping alone."

The congregation fell silent. I forgot about lunch. Only the babies continued to make a sound. Uncharacteristically subdued, the pastor went on to tell the story of "a bright, wonderful woman" who had been emotionally abandoned by her husband.

"At first she blamed herself. She thought if only she were a better wife, more attractive, more intelligent... then he would care," he said softly, his normally rich, booming voice reduced to little more than a whisper. "But none of it was her fault.

"Her husband was so caught up in his own work, his own self-worth, that he ignored her pleas to work on their relationship. Now, he wasn't a bad guy. In fact, he loved his wife. He came home every night. He never fooled around. But emotionally, he just wasn't available to her. Over the years, her loneliness, her pain, her isolation turned to resentment. It was only a matter of time....

"I realize I'm running late," he said, fighting back tears. "Let me conclude by saying that if you're married, make that relationship number two, right behind your relationship with Christ. Cherish it. Nurture it. Put time and energy into it. Be an active listener. Be generous with your companionship and intimacy. Communicate your feelings, and be open to hers. Give your spouse your very best, not what's left over. If not, you might end up full of regret and facing divorce... as I am today."

Without saying another word, he forced a smile and walked slowly from the altar to his office. The entire congregation, stunned at this revelation, remained seated for several minutes before quietly filing out.

I reached for my wife's hand, squeezing it tightly. "Thank you, Lord, for bringing us together," I prayed. "Allow me to never lose sight of my faith, my priorities, or the commitment of love I share with this lady."

I'll never forget that sermon.

IS HAPPINESS ON HOLIDAY?

Does it seem to you that happiness is on leave from your marriage? Does it seem that you share a bed with your spouse and little else? If so, then you've picked up the right book.

You knew when you got married that there would be choppy waters along the way. After all, your mother and father's union wasn't exactly perfect. You understood about commitment, about two people pulling together and all of that. But what if your partner has stopped pulling? Worse yet, what if your spouse is pushing you away?

One thing is for certain: This isn't the kind of marriage you signed up for. This isn't why you stood at the altar and confidently said, "I do." If you had wanted to feel alone, you would have stayed single.

I'm not saying that being alone doesn't have a place in our

lives. Even in the best of marriages, we need time to regroup, refocus, and rewind.

Certainly, there are many instances when Jesus sought solitude for prayer and rest. For example, Mark 1:35 tells us: "Very early in the morning, while it was still dark, Jesus got up, left the house and went off to a solitary place, where he prayed."

There are many forms of alone, such as alone by choice. You can be alone with your thoughts or alone in prayer. There are times to be left alone and times to let well enough alone. And there are times to stand bravely alone. But in a marriage, there is a big difference between being alone and feeling alone.

As Christians, marriage is supposed, be a legal and theological license to enjoy the fruits of our union. Marriage allows you to share simple pleasures, such as saying "good night" to the love of your life, the person God intended you to wed. Marriage allows you to enjoy, possibly for the first time, a loving, guiltless relationship. Marriage allows you to grow old contentedly and help spoil grandchildren until the day you go home to be with the Lord.

I've written this resource for people who feel like outsiders in their own marriages and whose relationships have become consumed with anger, pain, and resentment. This book is for people for whom the words *love, honor, and obey* may have been replaced with *dissatisfaction, disappointment, and dissolution.*

Be forewarned, repairing a damaged marriage isn't for the faint of heart. However, with equal portions of motivation, resolve, understanding, information, and prayer, I'm confident you can turn your marriage around.

Remember, a successful marriage isn't a remote dream, nor is it a maintenance-free possession. It's an honor to be worked for, achieved, and retained through continuing effort, consideration, and caring. Above all, remember that the first requirement for improving your relationship is a willingness to try. Without that spirit, few marriages would survive. With it, few would fail.

I'll ask only three things of you as you begin the all-important mission of restoring your marriage:

1. Make a commitment to change.

2. Keep a positive outlook.

3. Pray for God's assistance for both you and your spouse.

Speaking from years of experience, I can assure you that nothing will short-circuit success faster than negativity or stubbornly refusing to make changes. Before you turn one more page, do yourself a favor. Don't just think about change. Rather, DECIDE to change. In Matthew 19:26, Jesus looked at his disciples and said, "With man this is impossible, but with God all things are possible."

It's God's will that marriages succeed. Sadly, not enough people realize this. That partly accounts for the number of lonely couples, custody battles, communication snafus, unexpressed needs, unresolved conflicts, affairs, single parents, and divorce lawyers in our society today.

Remember, even if you aren't sure where your spouse stands regarding your marriage, YOU CAN SUCCEED!

This book will take you from the conceptual (your past) into the practical (your marriage). The problem-solving techniques you are about to experience in the following chapters are winners. They work! Step by step, you'll learn how to change the unchangeable, risk the unknown, and expect the unexpected. Above all, remember that God is unfailing in his pursuit of helping us repair our broken parts. With his unconditional love you can do it!

CHAPTER ONE

What Alone Can Mean

"Alone" can take many forms in our lives. There's alone in a crowd. Alone by choice. Alone with our thoughts. Alone in prayer. Time to be left alone. Time to stand bravely alone. And times when we should have let well enough alone.

For Shelly, whose husband agreed to counseling only after she threatened divorce, alone meant one word—*marriage.*

"The first few years were fine, even enjoyable," she told me during our initial counseling session. "Stan was thoughtful and affectionate. He'd plan special outings, open doors, bring home flowers, say 'I love you.' You know, do the little things. But he changed over time."

"Change? Right! I'm the one who changed, not you," Stan shot back sarcastically.

I told Stan there would be ample time for opposing views later. "Oh, I can see this is going to be a fair hearing," he said, rolling up his shirt sleeves. "Go ahead, dear!"

Shelly shrugged as if to say, "Do you see what I've got to put up with?"

"We never talk about anything important," she said, glancing nervously at her husband. "He comes home, grabs the remote and starts channel surfing until dinner time. And then he reads the paper throughout dinner while the kids and I discuss the day's events."

Stan tried to jump in again, but Shelly refused to yield the floor.

"He never leads the prayer," she continued. "And after dinner he can't wait to get back to his prized 'big screen,' which, by the way, cost us a fortune. And do you think he finds time to help the kids with their homework? No way! But he has plenty of time for the news and Letterman. He usually falls asleep on the couch. Some companion! I might as well be a single mom."

"Is that how you see it, Stan?" I asked.

"Oh, yeah! It's always me!" he said, removing his tie. "She fails to mention her nagging or that she finds time for everybody but me. And she wonders why we don't talk. Who wants to hear about problems all evening? Problems with the kids, the budget, tires for the minivan... whatever! She's a twenty-four-hour disaster channel. The TV is the only peace I get after a long, hard day. And she says she's feeling alone! By the way, the last time she wanted to make love, leisure suits were in style."

"Don't tell me you still have a lime-color polyester leisure suit hanging in your closet, too?" I said, hoping to defuse his anger. They looked at each other, and for the first time, exchanged smiles.

"All right, we know the two of you are unhappy," I said. "The question is, are you both willing to do whatever it takes to get this marriage back on track?" They both nodded. "Great! Something we can all agree upon."

It wasn't going to be easy, though. Years of ill will and loneliness had exacted a heavy toll on their relationship. Only Shelly's decision to stop suffering in silence and take action—with or without her husband—would set the stage for breaking this impasse.

How about you? How long have you suffered alone in silence? One year? Three years? Did it all begin somewhere between your first piece of wedding cake and your first heated discussion? It's sometimes helpful to step back and assess how you and your mate handled (or failed to handle) those "little" problems, disagreements, and misunderstandings early on in your marriage. How many of the same issues continue to plague your relationship today?

IN THE BEGINNING

Just as newlyweds are settling in for a long, happy marriage, unsettling and unexpected "his" and "her" complications arise. Little disagreements, such as watching twelve football games in a single weekend, control over the TV remote, raised toilet seats, housework, yardwork, in-laws, and shopping expeditions to the mall.

A certain number of awkward moments, misunderstandings, and disagreements should be expected in a new marriage. After all, both people are doing their best to adjust to a serious lifestyle alteration. And even if these issues aren't resolved as they pop up, the freshness and excitement of this new love keep small problems from becoming big ones.

But as the marriage progresses, more serious problems can enter the relationship. Even something as natural and pleasurable as sex can become a problem. She views him as a sex-starved testosterone monster. He views her as a conjugal visit. She can't even talk about sex without turning crimson. One day he brings home one of those "how to" books, which is quickly stashed under the bed. This from a couple who only a few years ago couldn't get enough of one another!

This wasn't how she visualized married life when he proposed. He was supposed to be sensitive, romantic, and attentive, not distant, secretive, and busy (but not too busy for weekend rounds of golf or hours of tinkering with his car).

And how does he view her? In the beginning, she couldn't do enough: home-cooked candlelight dinners, a different night-ie every evening. She even took a sincere interest in his work. Now it's microwave leftovers, boring flannel pajamas, and countless hours of volunteer work at the church. No wonder he spends so much time with his car!

And who could have known that money would create such friction in this relationship? He says she spends too much money on household necessities, but who is he kidding? He owns enough power tools to build a small city. If that's not bad enough, he paints little white outlines around each tool on his peg board. Heaven help her if she borrows a wrench and forgets to put it back. His lower lip quivers as he points to the white outline (resembling a crime scene) where the wrench used to be.

And worst of all, they don't talk anymore. They used to spend hours discussing their future together. Now it's mostly nonverbal communication, and most of it has become negative.

His communication: Grunting heavily.
Translation: "Bring me a cold drink."

Her communication: Hands on hips, bugged-out eyes.
Translation: "No, dear, we can't skip this family function! It's Christmas!"

His communication: Frantic arm waving.
Translation: "The remote is missing."

Her communication: Paint can and roller left by his side of the bed.
Translation: "Get out there and paint!"

Finally, after enduring just about all of the negativity they can stand, one spouse brings up the subject of marriage counseling, which is nearly always met with severe resistance.

His resistance to therapy: "Oh, you mean bonding, relating, empathizing, exploring my feminine side, getting in touch with my inner child. Forget it! Besides, it costs too much."

Her resistance to therapy: "As if that's going to help! Besides, we already go to church. Anyway, we all know who your *male* therapist is going to side with!"

Just when they thought life couldn't become more complicated, along comes an eight-pound, nine-ounce, crying, eating machine. Children are a special gift from God, but they demand three commodities that are in short supply in a struggling marriage: time, attention, and love. But this couple makes the best of it. At least neither spouse is totally alone anymore.

GOING IT ALONE

No question, we all need time alone. But many of us have been experiencing too much solitude, even when we are living with a marriage partner. Sadly, much of my counseling practice involves clients who feel just like you: married but very much alone.

Jenna, a friend of mine who was in the midst of a long and bitter divorce, gave me an insight into the sad irony of her situation: "When he proposed, he said we were 'a match made in heaven.' I should have demanded a receipt right then and there, while he was still on his knees!"

We laughed, but I could see her point. If matches really are made in heaven, why are there so many custody battles, communication breakdowns, unexpressed needs, unresolved conflicts, instances of spousal abuse, adulterous affairs, and divorce lawyers?

God may guide us in one direction or the other, but I believe it's our obligation to make our relationships work here on earth. But what if your partner, while physically under your roof, has emotionally checked out of the marriage?

Rescuing a marriage from the brink of breakdown is challenging enough for two motivated, mature adults. But how are you supposed to save your relationship single-handedly? Unfortunately, you may have no other choice. Let's face it, *you're* the one interested in marriage counseling, not your spouse. *You're* the one willing to accept your share of responsibility for the relationship.

While it's true that you may have to "go it alone" for the first few months, you also have the power to create positive change in your marriage and hopefully take your spouse along for the ride. In most cases, that means keeping your eyes open for what I call a "window of opportunity."

WHAT IS "THE WINDOW OF OPPORTUNITY"?

Whether it's hitting a golf ball, asking your boss for a raise, or preparing a five-course meal, the timing of your actions often means the difference between a dismal failure and a resounding success. The same holds true as you work to restore fulfillment to a lonely relationship. When your partner appears receptive to your efforts, the timing is right. I refer to this moment as a "window of opportunity."

For example, how wise would it be to ask for a raise after blowing a major deadline? Wouldn't it be better to create a more conducive environment for your request by waiting until after a favorable job evaluation?

But what if the timing is wrong? What if your spouse seems uninterested in your feelings or the idea of counseling? Well, then it's up to you to crack open that "window of opportunity" by *creating* your own good timing. If you don't, who will?

PAULETTE OPENS A WINDOW

If ever a couple needed a window of opportunity, it was Dean and Paulette. On two separate occasions, Dean had pulled the plug on marriage counseling when he felt the brunt of the blame being aimed squarely at him. He couldn't understand why both counselors focused on his controlling and selfish nature while ignoring Paulette's coldness and argumentativeness. Naturally, when his wife suggested a third attempt, he quickly shot down the idea.

So Paulette came to me for counseling by herself. That seemed only fitting to her since, in her mind, she had done everything else in her marriage by herself.

Paulette's initial concern was Dean's lack of cooperation in areas such as helping with household chores. She told me that his idea of assisting her was dragging the trash cans out to the curb once a week.

Paulette saw Dean's lack of effort as another example of how little he put into the marriage overall. The more resentful she became, the more she nagged him. The more she nagged, the more Dean resented her for trying to "mother" him, and the less he did to help.

With Dean's refusal to enter counseling at this time, the responsibility for initiating change fell squarely on Paulette's shoulders. The first step was to establish an initial goal. Paulette decided the goal was to try to get Dean back into marriage counseling. She also realized that unless things changed in the marriage, he'd never agree. Her challenge was to somehow soften his resistance to marriage counseling.

"You're going to need to reduce the amount of anger and resentment between you," I advised. Basically, I was asking Paulette to create her own window of opportunity by taking the first step of altering the negative pattern that was so ingrained in their marriage.

Paulette agreed to stop nagging and start being more loving to her husband. That meant doing things such as cooking more of his favorite meals, being more empathetic of his job stress and asking him more about his day. In essence, she would kill his resentfulness with kindness. The strategy worked. Midway through the second week, Paulette paged me to tell me that Dean would be attending the next counseling session.

Altering those old, negative patterns within your relationship is the best way to open the window of opportunity. Once you've accomplished that goal, the next move is to quickly prop it open long enough to make some headway. Whether the ultimate solution is found in marriage counseling, pastoral counseling, or simply the act of mutual kindness, little progress can be expected until a window of opportunity is created.

SOMETIMES I FEEL LIKE GETTING DIVORCED...

A cynical spouse once wrote, "Many a woman would get a divorce if she could do it without making her husband happy."

Some people view divorce as a panacea, an instant answer to the problems that have arisen in their marriages. Unfortunately, this is seldom the case. A significant number of those problems don't disappear after the divorce.

The situation is further complicated when children are a part of the relationship. Anyone who is contemplating divorce should remember this: If there are children involved, they *will* suffer damage as a result of the divorce.

"When children are involved, there is no such thing as divorce," said Carl Whitaker, an icon in the field of family therapy. No question about it, couples with kids should view divorce as a last resort.

I've yet to speak to any single parents who felt their lives had improved as a result of divorce. The reason? Divorce often means trading in one set of problems for another. For instance, a divorce isn't going to keep you from arguing frequently with your ex-spouse over parenting issues. If financial disputes currently trouble your marriage, do you think they will vanish with the sound of a judge's gavel?

So is divorce ever the answer? In certain cases, yes. In all my years of marriage counseling, I've recommended this drastic step on a few occasions that involved spousal or child abuse, drug or alcohol addictions, or repeated adulterous relationships. There are times when divorce is not only scripturally defensible but prudent as well.

Cases of chronic spousal abuse are both challenging and distressing. Christians are sometimes told by their pastors to return home, that a believer has an obligation to stay with his or her spouse, even if abuse occurs. However, if any pattern of physical or emotional abuse develops, a change in living arrangements is necessary. That means leaving the home, at least temporarily, while these issues are being professionally addressed.

A person has the right to say "NO" to abuse. If you are involved in a physically abusive relationship, a marriage repair book won't protect you from further abuse. Get out! Seek Christian counseling and proceed with the marriage repair work from a safe distance.

WHO'S RESPONSIBLE FOR MY HAPPINESS?

You might be saying, "If divorce isn't the answer, what can I do? I'm so unhappy in this marriage. I've tried everything I know to get my spouse to change, but nothing works!"

My goal here is to help you see what you *can* do. My goal is to provide you with the tools to help you feel less alone in your marriage and do what you can to rescue the relationship.

Most likely, you were motivated to pick up this book because you are unhappy in your marriage. But I have a question for you to think about: Is happiness a right or a privilege? Yes, it's mentioned prominently in the United States Constitution, as in "life, liberty, and the pursuit of happiness." But do you have an absolute, God-given right to happiness? I don't think so. Though happiness is always worth pursuing, nobody owes us happiness.

Let's start with two invaluable philosophies you may have missed during childhood.

1. *You are responsible for your own happiness.* Others may care, but they are largely incapable of creating or manipulating happiness in your world.

2. *People should have no more power to make us happy than they do to make us unhappy.*

God wants the best for us, which means he wants us to live in obedience to his ways and to be Christlike in our dealings with others. God doesn't guarantee our happiness, nor does he owe it to us. Jesus is a great example of this point. Do you think he was *always* happy while he was on this earth? Whenever I catch myself thinking I deserve to be happier, I remember how Christ died on the cross for the express purpose of taking the punishment that *I* really deserved.

Just where do we get the idea we deserve or have the *right* to happiness? Many of us were overindulged in childhood. We were taught to believe that our happiness was Mom and Dad's responsibility. Still others of us were neglected as children, deprived of not only happiness, but many of the basic necessities of life. We didn't have our needs or wants met, and now we are ready to collect.

There is nothing wrong with making an effort to be happy. The trouble comes when we allow ourselves to believe that any other person—including our spouses—is responsible for *making* us happy.

The pursuit of happiness is *your* responsibility. Happiness is a privilege earned through personal discipline and effort. The more effort you put into being happy, the greater your chances of achieving happiness.

TIME TO ACT

Once you realize that your happiness is your responsibility, you will be ready to take the next step in the healing of your marriage. You will be better equipped to make your marriage a happy one.

As you prepare to take the next step, consider these questions:

1. How much love are you willing to put back into the relationship?

2. How much effort are you willing to dedicate to the relationship?

3. *How much tolerance (grace) will you demonstrate when things don't exactly go according to plan?*

Keeping these things in mind, especially when the relationship is being severely tested, will ultimately strengthen your resolve to give more of yourself to the relationship.

A PLACE TO BEGIN

As your marriage has limped along, you've undoubtedly heard plenty of well-meaning advice. Insensitive suggestions, such as "Dump her," or "Give him a taste of his own medicine." Unrealistic advice, including "Give in and just take it," or "Whatever you do, don't divorce."

Perhaps your pastor advised you to confess your sins, pray harder (as if you weren't praying hard enough), or join yet another Bible study. That should straighten things out! Don't get me wrong. All of those ideas are very important parts of the Christian life. But they are only parts of what you need to do in order to restore your marriage.

Throughout this book, I emphasize that you *change what you can change within yourself.* By focusing on how you can make positive changes within yourself first, you may possibly spark positive changes in your spouse as well.

On the other hand, if you spend time trying to change your spouse, it will take longer for the marriage to heal, if it heals at all.

I recently counseled a woman who entered therapy for the sole purpose of getting her husband to pay more attention to her.

"Doctor, I'm not shy about making my feelings known," she said. "I've calmly asked my husband about showing more affection, about listening to my concerns and needs. But being calm doesn't work. It seems the only time he listens to me is when I explode. By that time it's too late, because we're both too upset."

I asked that she place herself in the role of an outsider and consider this question: "What percentage of your marital problems are attributable to you, and what percentage belongs to your spouse?" She thought for a minute: "Somewhere between one-third and one-half for each of us, I guess."

"What percentage of energy and attention have you focused on your husband's shortcomings versus your own?"

"I see your point," she said. "I probably spend about 95 percent of my time worrying about his faults."

Hers was a response typical of many others I've counseled.

SLICING THE "DYSFUNCTIONAL PIE"

Claiming your share of responsibility for the strife in your marriage is a significant and necessary step forward. To help you understand what areas fall within your power to change, I've developed a simple exercise called "Slicing the Dysfunctional Marriage Pie."

To do this exercise, start by taking a minute to draw your own circle (or pie) on a piece of paper. Next, divide the pie into eight equal slices. Now, in each of these slices, list one of the negative elements either you or your spouse has brought into your marriage: criticalness, distance, anger, victim-thinking, self-pity, pessimism. The list goes on, but you have to decide what goes in your pie.

After you have finished your pie, don't be surprised if a significant number of the slices are yours. If that is the case, don't be discouraged. Actually, that's good news! It means there is plenty of room for you to change. If none of the marriage problems belonged to you, then you would be powerless to make a meaningful difference. Again, *your goal should be to focus your attention only on what you can change.* Ignore, at least for now, your spouse's problems. Remember, they fall outside of your area of responsibility. But be encouraged—your changes will almost certainly influence your spouse to change as well.

Once you've finished your pie, save the drawing and refer to it often. Use it as a reference sheet as your important relational work proceeds. Take it one slice at a time. Select a slice—anger, for example—and work on that issue before tackling another piece of the pie.

It is important as you move through this process of self-change that you learn to be patient with yourself. Remember, your marriage didn't become a mess overnight, and you didn't develop your character flaws overnight, either! It will take time and commitment to make these changes. But with God's help, you can do it!

CHAPTER TWO

Taking Stock
of Your Life

For Coach Dennis, the "Surgeon of Swat," baseball had become more of a religion than a sport. The former-minor-league-shortstop-turned-major-league-batting-instructor zealously preached the science of hitting to rookies and superstars alike, and they all listened. If a player found himself slumping at the plate, he knew Dennis would find a cure for his ailing swing.

For Dennis, diagnosing a player's hitting woes meant watching countless hours of videotape. It also meant individual hitting instruction, sometimes long after practice had ended. And it meant coming home late night after night. In other words, while the team was having a phenomenal year hitting the baseball, his marriage was in a "major league" slump. His priorities were out in left field.

Finally, on the eve of a long road trip, his wife, Caren, announced that he had to make a choice: Make their marriage a priority or face the consequences.

The coach was shocked. Hadn't she always been his biggest fan? Hadn't she always welcomed him home with open arms at the end of every long road trip? Didn't she understand that this was his chance to finally make it at the major league level?

"After all these years, what's her problem?" he thought. "She knows that—at least during the season—baseball comes first."

Caren was tired of being put on the back burner during those long baseball seasons. She was tired of feeling alone and unappreciated. She was increasingly resentful of the time baseball was stealing from her and their two daughters. And she was especially sick of young players' wives and girlfriends continually asking, "What's your secret to a happy marriage?"

"If they only knew," she'd think.

Yes, Caren had expressed some discontent over the years. She and Dennis had even had a few discussions with their pastor. But she was always left with a feeling that her concerns weren't that important to her husband. After all, he was a baseball coach. And before anything could be resolved, Dennis was on an airplane, on a bus, in the middle of a road trip, or off hunting and fishing with the guys during the off-season.

Their entire relationship, she sadly concluded, was spent over the phone. She prayed that once his playing days ended he would finally become a full-time dad to their two daughters and a full-time husband to her.

When Dennis became more wrapped up in baseball than ever, Caren was ready to assume responsibility for her own happiness. For starters, Caren strongly suggested that they enter marriage counseling.

Like many men, Dennis initially vetoed any formal counseling sessions. He just didn't feel he was the one with a problem. Besides, Christians don't need counseling. They just need the Lord. But when Caren threatened to leave and take their daughters with her, he agreed to enter counseling. It was obvious at the outset of counseling that Dennis had one objective: getting his silently suffering wife to straighten out. In his mind, she was the one with a poor attitude. She was the one who had changed.

This one-sided way of thinking is typical of many people in marriage counseling. Their hidden agenda is simply to fix the other person. Usually, it's the man who wants his wife exorcised of emotional demons.

But if they stick with the counseling, one-sided thinkers begin to see both sides. They learn that they have a distorted view of marriage, a view that was often formed during childhood. In Dennis' case, it was revealed that his father had always been emotionally distant from his mother. Dennis was unconsciously following the very same script in his own marriage.

Dennis realized he had to change his priorities. He agreed to spend more time with his family and less time analyzing videotape after hours. With his new insight, the couple began making adjustments that would improve their marriage. Their long marital slump was ending.

Dennis' case isn't unusual. I've discovered that many couples find themselves drifting apart, feeling alone and emotionally let down for no apparent reason. If that describes your marriage, then perhaps it's time for you to ease off the gas pedal and coast in for what I call a "Priority Pit Stop."

A PRIORITY PIT STOP

When I use the term "Priority Pit Stop," I mean taking time to set priorities to determine what the *important* aspects are in your marriage relationship. And what are the *essential* ones?

To help you set your priorities, pencil out a two-column checklist of the current priorities in your life. In one column, list only the *important* things in your life. In the other column, jot down the *essential* things. Highlight any item that you suspect may be out of balance, showing wear, or in need of a major overhaul.

The following model will undoubtedly differ from yours, but the goal remains the same: to strike a balance between the important and essential things in your life.

Important	Essential
Making more money.	Your relationship with Jesus.
Getting ahead in business.	Your relationship with your wife.
Hobbies and recreation.	Quality time with your children.
Spending time with friends.	Quality time as a family.
Acquiring property and things.	

If your priority pit stop reveals that you are placing too much emphasis on the *important* rather than the *essential* areas in your life, your marriage may need a tune-up, or it may be time for you to authorize some major professional work.

The following checklist has proven to be extremely useful in helping me to order the priorities in my life, especially when they seem to be shifting in one direction or another

1. My relationship with God.
2. My relationship with my wife.
3. My relationship with my children.
4. My ministry.

How does it compare with yours? Remember, it should be used as a starting place only. Your own priority checklist will require honesty, commitment, and prayer to establish and maintain.

ARE YOU NUMBER ONE ON YOUR PRIORITY LIST?

Selfishness is the most common symptom associated with out-of-balance relationships. This is often just a matter of adjusting to life with another person. Remember when you were single? If you wanted to go to the movies, you went. If you wanted to sleep until noon, you slept. As a single person, you had the luxury of tending exclusively to your own needs and wishes.

But as husbands and wives, our lives have changed. We have another person who depends on us for love and support, who in turn gives us love and support. It's a wonderful arrangement. But when we slip into selfish behavioral modes, our priorities get blurred and our lives shift out of balance. I'm not saying you shouldn't care for yourself, but do so in concert with the wishes of God and the needs of those you love.

TOM'S PRIORITIES

A pastor I know needed a favor. Two new members—Barbara and Tom—were having serious marital problems. He asked if I could give them a call.

"Greg, Barbara sounded very upset on the phone," the pastor told me. "Seems her husband isn't just a workaholic, he's also becoming more and more verbally abusive. If it's not too much trouble, could you give her a call?"

Not surprisingly, Barbara was extremely receptive to marriage counseling, but said her husband wanted no part of it.

"He doesn't want to spend the money," she said. "Besides, he blames me for our problems. He thinks I should try harder to be a good wife."

After I assured her there would be no charge, Tom grudgingly agreed to join her, "for one session only!" (Why is it that people will spend thousands of dollars on divorce attorneys, child support, alimony—not to mention the thousands they lose in property settlements—but won't invest a dime in counseling?)

Barbara timidly framed her concerns, her husband sitting with his arms crossed and a scowl on his face. "I'm on edge all of the time around him," she said. "I'm supposed to jump when he speaks. If he asks me to do some typing, it comes across like an order. OK, he pays me for the typing, and it's more than the allowance I used to get to run the household and take care of the kids. But his attitude... I don't feel like his wife; I feel like an employee, a nanny for his two children."

Tom was silent as Barbara spoke—except for the sound of gnashing teeth. When I asked him about his thoughts, he was more than ready to unload them on me and his wife.

"Yeah, I'm a real taskmaster," he said sarcastically. "Sure, she does some typing. Big deal, a couple hours a day. The rest of the day is hers. And how does she act? By not making love to me anymore, and by dragging me into counseling!"

This was my window of opportunity to illustrate the seriousness of his situation.

"Tom, how do you feel about being a single parent? How about child support and alimony for the next twelve years?" Before he could answer, I asked him if he could still afford to live in a nice house after a divorce settlement. Then I asked him if he still loved his wife, or if she was simply a convenience.

"That's a laugh! You think she's going leave me because we're having a few little problems?" Tom turned to Barbara for reassurance, but she just looked away. He had his answer—and not the one he wanted!

Barbara had wedged open a window of opportunity by seeking professional help. She could just as easily have walked out of the marriage and taken the children with her. Instead, she had the courage to stay and fight for her dream of a loving relationship and a good Christian home. Without that step, Tom surely would have paid the price for ignoring God's admonishment to all of us: To love the Lord with all your heart and to love your neighbor (including your spouse) as you love yourself.

Like Tom, many of us lose sight of the priorities and high ideals we carried into marriage. How about you? Have you suddenly lost track? Or have you known the truth for a long time? If you're tired of being angry, burned out, and trapped in feelings of unhappiness and loneliness, then read on.

As we address key emotional issues that plague many marriages, watch for symptoms that may affect your own marriage.

A ONE-WAY STREET

Does your spouse seem uninterested in you and your needs or distant from you, emotionally and physically? If so, you may be involved in what I call a "one-sided" relationship. In order to help you assess your relationship and what changes need to be made, let's first examine and define some of the more prevalent characteristics of one-sided relationships.

Apathy—One spouse doesn't appear as interested in understanding or meeting the other's needs. This triggers negativity in the relationship that often snowballs out of control.

Distance—An emotional state of mind where physical and emotional distance is created out of fear of intimacy. Distance is facilitated through a number of hiding styles. Some of these styles are obvious, while others are more difficult to spot. Here are just a few: Anger, manipulation, control, workaholism, or obsessive and compulsive traits such as overeating, excessive cleaning, or drugs and alcohol.

Devaluing—Just about all needs in a marriage are legitimate. You may not be able to meet them all, but that doesn't reduce their legitimacy. Devaluing comes in when one spouse discounts, ignores, or refuses to meet the other spouse's needs. This is often done in a "tit-for-tat" way. In other words, "You don't meet my needs, I don't meet yours."

Distrust—Good relationships provide each spouse with an implied sense that their emotional needs will be met. When legitimate needs go unmet or ignored, trust is lost, along with intimacy. Trust naturally erodes when violations of trust come into play. The trust restoration process involves both spouses being more faithful to the needs being entrusted to them.

Anger and resentment—If you are involved in a one-sided relationship, anger and resentment will most certainly become a part of it. We'll discuss these two emotions in greater depth in later chapters. For now, understand that they are protective or defensive hiding styles. Anger and resentment are the mind's way of protecting itself from further pain.

WHERE DO YOU STAND IN YOUR MARRIAGE?

Now, let's take a little true-or-false quiz. Go with the first answer that flashes in your brain. That's how you'll find out if you are in a one-sided relationship.

1. I believe I try harder than my spouse does to make our marriage work.
   [] true []false

2. Frequently, we don't even sleep together in the same bedroom.
   [] true []false

3. I feel as if my needs don't count for much as far as my spouse is concerned.
   [] true []false

4. I often feel as if I've lost the loving feelings I used to have for my spouse.
   [] true []false

5. I've lost some respect for my spouse.
   [] true []false

6. I sometimes wonder if divorce is just around the corner.
   [] true []false

7. I sometimes think things might be better for me if we divorced.
   [] true []false

8. If it weren't for my religious faith, I would ask for a divorce.
   [] true []false

9. We argue now more than ever.
   [] true []false

10. My spouse seldom, if ever, says he or she loves me.
    [] true []false

11. We spend very little time doing fun things together.
    [] true []false

12. If given the choice, I'd rather spend time with others than with my spouse.
    [] true []false

13. I am quick to apologize, but my spouse seldom admits he or she is wrong.
    [] true []false
14. When we're together, we don't seem to have much to talk about.
    [] true []false
15. I think my spouse is too critical of me.
    [] true []false
16. I wish my spouse were more romantic.
    [] true []false
17. It seems as if I'm always the one to plan trips and dates.
    [] true []false
18. I am frustrated with our sex life.
    [] true []false
19. Sometimes I feel as though I'm last on my spouse's priority list.
    [] true []false
20. My spouse would prefer that I be quiet and submissive.
    [] true []false
21. I sometimes feel as if I don't have the right to say "no" to my spouse or to disagree.
    [] true []false
22. We've grown apart, and I wonder if we're just incompatible now.
    [] true []false
23. My spouse's needs are probably more important than my own.
    [] true []false
24. Sometimes I say "yes" when I want to say "no" to my spouse.
    [] true []false
25. My spouse doesn't listen to me as well as I listen to him or her.
    [] true []false
26. No one *really* knows how unhappy I am in my marriage.
    [] true []false

27. I may have gotten overly involved with my kids out of the lack of connection with my spouse.
[] true []false
28. My spouse probably has more control over me than he or she should.
[] true []false
29. I don't really look forward to intimate moments with my spouse or sometimes I avoid them.
[] true []false
30. On occasion I find myself attracted to someone of the opposite sex who seems kind or who has paid attention to me.
[] true [] false
31. I feel I can talk to others about my problems more easily than I can to my spouse.
[] true [] false
32. My spouse used to put more effort into talking with me and tending to my needs.
[] true [] false
33. I feel bad about this, but sometimes I think our family runs more smoothly when my spouse is away.
[] true [] false

If you answered "true" to ten or more of these statements, then you are no doubt feeling alone in your relationship. If that is the case, don't despair! I believe that a window of opportunity will present itself in your marriage if you are willing to look for it.

CRUISE CONTROL CAN BE HAZARDOUS

After years of marriage, have you gone from cheerleader to critic? Supporter to detractor? Lover to loather, seemingly overnight? Has your relationship gone from romantic walks along the shore to evenings at home while your spouse works late or is out with friends?

As time goes on, you become more and more resentful. And why? Because you're in a one-sided relationship! Your spouse doesn't lift a finger to help improve matters, either. It may take a Herculean effort, but be patient. At this point in the restoration process, it isn't necessary that your spouse match the energy you are pouring into the marriage. Remember, your marriage didn't grow distant overnight.

In a good marriage each spouse stays focused and gives attention to the other's needs. I've come to understand that the phrase "We just grew apart" translates to "We put our marriage on cruise control and the rest is history."

Let me illustrate: Let's say you leave work, get on the freeway and set your cruise control for 70 mph. A mile later, you're stopped by a police officer, who issues you a ticket for doing 70 in a 55 mph zone.

No problem, you reason. You'll just go to traffic school and have this indiscretion erased from your record. And the plan works, for now....

On the way home from traffic school, you jump back onto the freeway and set your cruise control for 70 again. The same officer who pulled you over the first time stops you and gives you another ticket. This time you have to pay the $200 fine.

Grumbling every mile of the way home from the courthouse, you again set the cruise control for 70 and guess what? That same officer pulls you over. "Here's another ticket. Have a nice day!"

This time you go before the judge. You try to explain that it's not your fault. After all, you only set the cruise control. The car did the rest. Unimpressed with your defense, the judge instructs you to pay a $500 fine, cautioning that one more speeding violation will cost you your license and eight weekends of picking up trash along the freeway in a pretty orange vest. His final word of encouragement: "Disconnect the cruise control!" You do, and your problems with the law become a thing of the past.

This parable illustrates how we often don't take control of our lives until it's either too late or someone in authority holds a gavel over our heads. The message? If you suspect you are in a one-sided relationship, don't wait until the consequences for your actions are staring you in the face before you make changes. Start now to disconnect the cruise control in your marriage.

WISHFUL THINKING?

A pivotal first step to making positive change in your marriage is to discover the root cause of the emotional distance. Without blaming, take an honest inventory of your marriage and attempt to identify and differentiate between your legitimate emotional needs and your wishes. Most marital ills can be traced directly to unmet or unspoken needs or wishes.

Consider this: What happens when your emotional needs are denied? You experience severe pain. What happens when your desires fail to materialize? There's discomfort. Be careful not to confuse the two when delving into this important facet of your marriage.

When a person's communicated needs are stifled or unmet by his or her spouse, the relational net worth of the marriage plummets. Terrified of risking further rejection, husbands and wives often stop communicating about what they need from their spouse. Consequently, anger and loneliness consume the marriage, as neither spouse sees his or her needs met.

Men and women were never intended to be totally autonomous! Since the day God created us, it was expected that we would honor, respect, and at least try to meet each other's needs.

The question for you to ask is: What emotional needs are legitimate and fall within your responsibility, and what needs are completely out of your hands—or your spouse's for that matter? If you've been keeping your legitimate needs hidden from your spouse, it's not too late to identify, acknowledge, and communicate those needs.

Before you try to identify your needs, let me clarify the difference between needs and wishes. A typical wish list looks something like this:

"I wish he were stronger in his faith."

"I wish I had more money."

"I wish my husband was more like my girlfriend's husband."

"I wish we lived in a bigger house."

"I wish my wife understood me better."

Wishful thinking begins in childhood. Remember your first bicycle? You were elated until your best friend received a bigger, better bike. Possibly for the first time, you wished for something somebody else had. You didn't *need* it; you simply *wanted* it.

Many, if not most, adults continue to engage in this type of thinking. By doing so, however, to a degree we lose control over our own lives.

Another problem with wishful thinking is that it causes us to enter a frame of mind that calls for comparisons with what others have. But needs don't rely on comparisons. Needs are things in our lives that we must have met in order to be happy and healthy.

A typical need list looks like this:

I need to feel loved.

I need to feel respected and valued.

I need to feel cared for.

I need to feel in control of my life.

I need to feel safe.

I need to feel freedom.

Whenever we wager our happiness on wishes (secret longings and desires), it only distracts us from reaching our goals. So be sure not to confuse wishes or desires with needs. Allow your spouse, through loving communication, the chance to meet your specific needs.

IDENTIFYING YOUR NEEDS

We are truly needy creatures, which God understood completely when he said, "It's not good for man to be alone." God had already given Adam dominion over the creation, but that couldn't satisfy the man's God-given need for a relationship.

Ironically, when people feel alone in their marriages, their first response is often to isolate themselves from their spouse. It's an age-old behavioral reflex. For example, when God confronted Adam and Eve after the original sin, their insecurity and shame drove them into hiding, rather than to their Creator.

People *still* flee with their needs to avoid rejection, so I guess not much has changed since the days of Adam and Eve. But instead of ducking behind the shrubbery, they hide behind ten-hour work days, gambling, overspending, extramarital affairs, drugs and alcohol, food, overparenting, and excessive volunteering. These things are often ways to keep from appearing needy around spouses who are seemingly unwilling to meet our needs.

Is it time for you to take inventory of what you need from your spouse in order to feel happier in your marriage? Go back and review the "need" and "wish" list, and determine how many examples represent areas of dissatisfaction in your relationship. How many of these things contribute to your sense of loneliness?

On a sheet of paper, make a list of the five most important needs that you want to make known to your spouse. When you're finished, carefully examine your list to be sure these are indeed the five most important items affecting your marriage. Don't show them to your spouse just yet. At some point, this list will become an integral part of the reparative process in your marriage. When that time arrives, ask your spouse for a corresponding list of his or her needs.

JILL'S STORY

Jill's marriage was in deep trouble, and divorce looked like a sure thing. As so often is the case, marriage counseling was a last resort. Naturally, her husband was oblivious to his role in the problem. But he was willing to put the divorce on hold while she entered therapy to be "cured."

I began by asking Jill to list three needs that were not being met in her marriage, needs that, if her husband were willing, would make their marriage better. Then I suggested that Jill ask her husband to go through the same exercise.

Some couples have kept their needs hidden so long that they have difficulty writing them down or expressing them. For these people, needs represent emotional pain, the pain that comes from a relationship with someone who doesn't seem to care about their needs. Some people react like children, as in "I don't need that stupid old doll anyway."

But Jill didn't have any trouble completing her "needs" list.

"What about Dick's list?" I asked.

"Get this, Greg," she said with a look of exasperation. "He finishes the list and hands it to me like a grocery list I'm supposed to fill. I don't think so! He never even asked me about my list."

"So, how did you respond? Wait, don't tell me. You graciously thanked him for his effort and asked him if he would like to discuss your list of needs, right?"

She laughed and admitted that the subject never came up. She was so upset that she tossed both of the lists into the garbage, only to fish them out the next day.

I explained to Jill that she had missed a "window of opportunity" and a chance to reopen the lines of communication in a loving way.

"I've got to be honest, Jill. You acted like a little girl. You took your doll and went home."

"I failed the test, didn't I?" she asked.

"Actually, I could have coached you guys through the exercise, warned you about unrealistic expectations and reacting defensively. But you needed to see yourselves. Now we can more openly evaluate your answers."

So what was on the two lists? Jill wrote that she needed:

1. *To feel like the most important person in her husband's life, after God.*
2. *To have the assurance and security that her husband wouldn't go outside of the marriage for intimacy.*
3. *To feel loved and to be intimate with her husband without it necessarily having to lead to sex.*

Her husband had listed that he needed:
1. *More respect.*
2. *More physical intimacy.*
3. *To feel more important in his wife's life than the kids, work, and other things.*

What was so ironic is that Jill and Dick produced similar lists! They both needed to feel significant, experience more real intimacy, and have a sense of belonging. I've seen this often in my counseling practice. Though a husband's need list is usually more direct than a wife's, the underlying theme is usually the same: both express a need for emotional security.

Armed with this new insight, Jill was able to take the reparative process to the next level. This time, at the bottom of her list, she wrote to her husband, "Please ask me about my list of needs."

When they sat down together and examined each other's lists, they were amazed. How could they have shared so many of the same needs, yet failed so miserably at meeting them? Both were so preoccupied with their own needs—and how they weren't being addressed—that they were frozen in their own pain and disappointment. This is an example of what I call an emotional stare out. Neither spouse was willing to give an inch, and both felt isolated and alone. (More on "stare-outs" in chapter seven.)

The next step for Jill and Dick was to discuss and prioritize their lists so they could determine what was the most pressing need for each of them. For Jill, it was the need to feel like the most important person in Dick's life. For Dick, it was to feel more respected. Obviously, each wanted to be held in higher esteem by the other.

Jill asked her husband, "What can I do to help you feel more respected in our marriage?" Dick's eyes widened. It was the moment he had been waiting for. Yet, all he could say was, "Gee, I don't know." Dick had spent so much time wishing to have his needs met that he had forgotten what he really needed from his relationship.

But with Jill's help, Dick was able to verbalize his needs. And almost instantly, he felt more respected, simply because she was listening to him. Don't overlook this insight: *When someone you love tells you what they need, your correct response is <u>always</u> to validate their need and to acknowledge it positively.* You don't necessarily have to agree, or hustle to fill that need. But you should acknowledge the need and place it on the table for discussion. If Jill had criticized, disagreed, or minimized Dick's stated need, he would have been much more likely to hide his future needs, and understandably so.

They were now on the right track. Jill and her husband had successfully identified their needs in the marriage and had communicated them to each other. They were learning to move from a "wish state" (I wish he'd ask me...) to an "expressive state" (I need you to ask me... I need you to hear me...). In so doing, they had jointly opened the window of opportunity in their marriage.

Remember, a successful couple listens, acknowledges, and honors the needs of one another. They are reliable trustees for each other's emotions, dreams, and expectations.

PLAYING HIDE-AND-SEEK WITH HER NEEDS

Wives often enter what I call a "need cycle" when husbands don't acknowledge or meet their needs. Does the following scenario sound familiar?

Step 1: Hiding. She feels hurt, frustration, and anger over her unfulfilled needs.

Step 2: Seeking. She finds passive or hostile ways to express her anger, disappointment, and frustrations over the relationship. She may do this to punish her husband for not seeing to her present needs and to manipulate him into better tending to her future needs.

Step 3: Hiding. When he responds in anger to what he perceives as manipulation or pushiness, she sees him as even more unsafe to express her needs to and withdraws and hides emotionally.

Step 4: Seeking. When an opportunity arises, she checks to see if he is any better at attending to her needs. When she finds that nothing has changed, she returns to step 2, and the cycle repeats itself.

PLAYING HIDE-AND-SEEK WITH HIS NEEDS

Husbands also enter the need cycle when wives don't acknowledge or meet their needs. The details may be different, but the cycle is fundamentally the same.

Step 1: Hiding. He feels disconnected, unimportant, and abandoned over the lack of connection in the relationship. He hides emotionally, often spending long hours at the office or in recreation. This is a form of self-protection from future hurts.

Step 2: Seeking. His discontent turns to anger and resentment over his unmet needs and he takes opportunities to emotionally punish her for what he perceives as her lack of caring. He somehow feels that he can manipulate or coerce her into better meeting his needs.

Step 3: Hiding. When his inappropriate attempts to have his needs met are returned with hostility or lack of concern, he goes back into hiding, only to occasionally venture out to see if she is any safer than before.

Step 4: Seeking. When he sees that the situation hasn't changed, he repeats step 2, and the cycle begins again.

As you can see, both need cycles involve a complex combination of hiding and seeking, which is driven by hurt, disappointment, and frustration.

BREAKING THE NEED CYCLE

Breaking the need cycle starts with acknowledging your involvement in the process. Denying that you are a willing participant in the hide-and-seek scenario will only entrench you in this destructive pattern. Resist the temptation to think: "That sure sounds like my spouse, but I don't see myself in the cycle." Sorry, it takes two to cycle!

If you intend to progress in your relationship, you're going to have to take a risk. This means dropping your guard in order that your spouse will drop his or hers. Be more open to dialogue with your spouse. It's not going to be easy, but here are some guidelines:

1. *Don't be distant.*

2. *Don't punish.*

3. *Don't ignore or minimize either your needs or the needs of your spouse.*

4. *Ask for your needs to be met.*

5. *Ask your spouse what his or her needs are.*

You don't have to slay all of these marriage-killers at once. Just making a positive dent in several areas—such as showing a sincere interest in your mate's needs—will establish a foundation from which to build.

CHAPTER THREE

Learning from
Your Family Script

The buzzards, along with several divorce attorneys, were already circling Holly's seven-year marriage. She was feeling so lonely and alienated from her husband that divorce looked like the only answer. As a last resort, she decided to make an appointment with a Christian counselor, not to open a window of opportunity but to give her the strength and validation to leave.

Holly arrived at my office early, and wasted no time launching into her husband, John, who made his living selling promotional items. "He's devoid of drive," she said. "Don't get me wrong, selling promotional items is OK. But he's not interested in his future. Our future.

"He'd rather leave the office, pull our daughter out of day care early and take her to the park or dance practice. I'm glad he spends time with her, but where are his priorities? Whenever a good business opportunity comes along, he bails."

Holly explained how she had tried everything to coax her husband up the corporate ladder, including signing him up for night school without his knowledge. "I've even taped employment ads to the back of his cereal box. All he cares about is the prize inside!"

I reminded Holly that she must have had some good reasons

for selecting a friendly Irish setter over an aggressive pitbull for a husband. Her expression went blank. My next question finally touched a nerve: "Do you think it's possible that your controlling style might be driving him away and causing you to feel angry and alone at the same time?"

"Controlling? That's funny," she said. "I can't force him to do anything. He's either at his bowling league or doing things with our daughter. He's never around."

It didn't matter that John was an excellent father and that he was warm and caring. That he worked steadily and that he still loved his wife didn't seem to make a difference to Holly. In her eyes, John had failed his patriarchal duties as main breadwinner. And all because he wasn't interested in becoming the next Donald Trump!

To start with, Holly needed to come to terms with her own character flaws. Up until now she had placed all of the blame on her husband and failed to see her own role in their problems. As we talked, what emerged was a picture of a controlling, moody, and perfectionist wife who was driving her husband away. I asked her, "I understand that John has his share of problems, but aren't you exhausted by always being the responsible one, always being the decision-maker, and the person in control?"

A flood of tears answered my question.

A number of fuzzy assumptions about Holly came into sharp focus in later sessions. For example, Holly was thrust into the role of what I term "the Controlling Superstar" by her alcoholic mother early in her childhood. As a result, many of the household responsibilities fell on her small shoulders.

Holly recalled, as a five-year-old, holding the bottle for her baby sister. She remembered how surprised she was by the praise and attention she received.

"People were astounded," she said. "They were always saying, 'You're such a big girl. Your mom is so lucky to have a little helper around the house.'"

Before long, Holly was changing diapers, making sure "the kids" did their chores, getting them ready for school, assisting with homework, and even disciplining them when they misbehaved. Holly had mastered her superstar role in the family. Sadly, that didn't leave much time for a happy, carefree childhood.

For Holly, identifying her personality pattern and what caused it was an important step in turning her empty and lonely marriage around.

FOLLOWING A SCRIPT

If your childhood was adapted for the big screen, how would it rate? Would it be an enduring cinematic classic or box office bomb?

Let's face it, our early childhood scripts were basically out of our hands. We were tossed a few measly pages, expected to learn our lines and told to stick to the script. Would it be a starring part or a cameo appearance? Would we be the romantic lead or the silly sidekick? Were you the hero or the villain? What if the best roles were already cast, snapped up by a superstar brother or annoyingly talented and pretty older sister? Much is up to the directors (our parents) and the cast (our siblings). We can't even hire a new agent!

Most of us were lucky growing up. We had parents who lovingly directed us through childhood while endowing us with a positive sense of self and respect for others. Others, however, were negatively influenced by alcoholics, abusers, or parents too busy making a buck to make us a childhood. The old saying remains valid today: "We're all products of our environment." Genetics may pen the opening pages, but environment dominates the script.

But I have some good news! Playing a lackluster, frightened, or lonely role in your childhood doesn't mean you're under a lifetime contract. You have the power to scrap the script and edit the ending. Happy endings have a nice ring, don't they?

YOUR FAMILY SYSTEM

Families and churches have two very important things in common: Both operate at peak efficiency when each member has the same positive objectives. Paul says in 1 Corinthians 1:10 (Living Bible), "Let there be real harmony so that there won't be splits in the church. I plead with you to be of one mind, united in thought and purpose."

A healthy family system promotes harmony, reduces tension and maintains stability, while providing a safe place to grow and mature. But how many of us were raised in a perfect family system?

I've gathered together a small ensemble of characters, some of whom might have performed in your childhood. As the curtain rises, see if you can identify with any of the roles. Were you the Superstar, the Sidekick, the Scapegoat, the Victim, the Forgotten Child, or the Comic? If you're feeling alone in your marriage, there's a good chance you've played—or are still playing—one or more of these roles.

Note: As you review this ensemble of characters, look for personality traits and attitudes that relate *not only* to you but to your spouse as well. See how these roles have influenced your own marriage. In order to select the right course of action to improve your relationship—especially if you're on your own for now—it's essential to understand just what type of characters you and your spouse are dealing with.

THE SUPERSTAR

One child generally rises through the sibling ranks in the family system to gain top billing as what I call "the superstar." Legends in their own homes, superstars grow up to a "Hallelujah Chorus" of glowing remarks. They are considered wonderful, responsible, mature, considerate, talented, smart, and physically attractive. The more dysfunctional the family, the larger their name appears on the family marquee.

Superstars learn to be perfectionists early in life. When they were good, there was attention and approval. As children, when they fell short of the perceived mark, there was disapproval. This placed the budding superstar on a high-performance track in order to maintain his minimum daily allowance of love, attention, and acceptance.

Superstars are generally rigid, "black-and-white" thinkers. In other words, they see things as either all good or all bad, a success or failure. There's no "wiggle room" for mistakes, no margin for error.

Being "just good enough" doesn't cut it in the superstars' world. Instead of being grateful for God-given gifts, superstars anguish over the talents and skills they lack. They struggle—and sometimes stumble—trying to meet their own impossibly high standards. As a result, they may freeze at the starting blocks in fear of losing the race.

Superstars may not be "natural born leaders," but they grow into the role through countless hours of dress rehearsals. Worst of all, they start believing their own press clippings. While playing cops and robbers, guess who wears the badge? If ambushed in play by a bazooka-wielding sibling, will they play by the rules and fall dead, or protest loudly, "You cheated! And besides, you missed me!"

Accomplished control freaks, adult superstars would rather have a tooth extracted than relinquish the reigns of control. The mere mention of carpooling sends shivers down their spines. They maintain a death-grip on the TV remote, and they choose the restaurant or vacation destination.

So it's no shock that superstar adults have trouble being team players or following instructions, especially from those they deem less capable, which is just about everybody. They also find it nearly impossible to form working partnerships with their spouses, since there's no room for anyone else in their lives.

A superstar lives by the motto, "It's my way or the highway." He's never heard saying, "It's my fault, honey. I was wrong." If you spot a superstar smiling after making a mistake, it's because he just thought of someone to blame it on. In other words, he's terrific at "passing the buck."

Addicted to the limelight, superstars are convinced nobody would love or respect them offstage. As a result, they have trouble relaxing or being themselves. They prefer keeping their adoring fans—even their spouses—at a safe distance. You see, they have a tightly guarded secret: insecurity.

The family superstar is often a "worry wart." It's common for the superstar to obsess about negative things, such as crime, work, money, security, cleanliness, and world peace. In their hopeless search for guarantees in life, superstars are usually governed by—and bogged down by—an endless morass of rules, lists, and schedules. In fact, they often forget what interested them about a given activity in the first place. Sadly, work often supplants relationships in their lives.

As you might imagine (or already know), superstars are a real challenge in married life because they are so intolerant of others, especially those seemingly more carefree and less driven to succeed. They secretly (and sometimes openly) see "normal" people as sloppy, unmotivated, and undisciplined.

Superstars may seem confident—even egotistical—but their self-esteem is fragile at best. It hangs precariously on the positive comments of others. Amid thunderous ovation, they feel good about themselves. If those cheers turn to boos, however, they're devastated. If you have the nerve to offer constructive criticism, they'll view you as the enemy or a traitor.

When it comes to making comparisons, the superstar is without rival. Be it appearance, status, money, cars, watches, houses, spouses, children, or pets. You name it, and superstars compare it. Everything becomes a yardstick, a means by which to measure success and failure. That is also how they reinforce their own unhappiness and justify their obsession with reaching the top.

Interestingly enough, some superstars grow weary of always playing to the crowd. Face it, it's a high-stress, tiring job. They might even quit their job, buy a sports car, buy into a mid-life crisis, or have an affair—all in an effort to discover how the "other half" (perceived as irresponsible and spontaneous) lives.

Family superstars aren't always as easily recognized as you might think. For example, they may be so compulsively perfectionist that they appear to lack discipline—always starting and stopping projects (sometimes several at a time) without completing even one. On the other hand, the more perfectionist superstars may focus on one project at a time and manage it to death, never finishing it to their own satisfaction.

Superstars seldom feel satisfied in their marriages. How can they? There's no way they could possibly reap the same praise and adoration from their spouses that they soaked up during childhood. Not in a committed, mature relationship such as marriage. Eventually, the superstar's partner grows weary of constantly giving, while receiving little in return. As the spouse pulls back emotionally, the superstar once again feels vulnerable, insecure, and alone. He or she still craves the applause.

THE SIDEKICK

In football, he's the water boy; at the office, the "go-fer." He's framed in murder mysteries, ignored by leading ladies, and no self-respecting western hero worth his spurs would be without one. Neither would a truly dysfunctional family. I'm talking about "the sidekick."

You can easily spot a sidekick, because they:

1. Are always the ones with hands raised, volunteering to head up church projects.
2. Take other moms' turns driving the car pool, even if it's inconvenient.
3. Work in the church nursery (with no rotation schedule) because nobody else would.
4. Run errands for others, way beyond the call of duty.

Mopping up everybody else's mess is a sidekick's role. Sidekicks try to keep the peace, see both sides, and do the dishes—whatever it takes to keep everybody happy. Sure, the sidekick may have to suffer a few "slings and arrows" intended for the superstar, but that's his role.

Sidekick kids aren't born; they're made. Generally the second or middle child, the sidekick often comes from family systems where issues of scapegoating, emotional distancing, or abusiveness are part of a dysfunctional mix.

Unfortunately, the sidekick often evolves into the classic codependent adult. With no real sense of self, the sidekick's time is consumed with adapting to the emotions of others. As a codependent, the sidekick doesn't view himself as an equal partner in marriage. His role was, and continues to be, to support, please, and stay out of the superstar's way. The problem is, the sidekick generally dislikes this subordinate position. He'd rather be treated as an equal, appreciated and respected. Unfortunately, he just never learned how to earn that place in life.

There is a big difference between the way sidekicks see themselves and the way others see them. Unfortunately, what the sidekick likes to think of as character strengths are only weaknesses in disguise.

How Sidekicks See Themselves	How Others See Them
Generous	Easily taken advantage of
Selfless	No sense of identity
Supportive	Weak
Flexible	Indecisive
A best friend	A follower
Easygoing	Insignificant
Popular	Popular, but often a nuisance

As I've mentioned, sidekicks shrink in the presence of power and authority. They're comfortable taking the backseat within a family system and within a marriage. They shun the spotlight, remaining less than content, but compliant within the relative obscurity of a supporting role.

Again, there comes a time when most adult sidekicks come face-to-face with feelings of resentment. Tired of being subjugated, unappreciated, and undervalued by their domineering spouses, they eventually assert themselves. If not afforded that freedom, the sidekicks will distance themselves from the relationship.

Since many sidekicks come from broken homes or insecure family systems, they often brood needlessly over the specter of divorce or separation in their adult lives. A sidekick is deathly afraid of being alone, yet he naturally distances himself from those who love him. Left unresolved, these issues of abandonment may lead to even more passive behavior until his spouse—once attracted to the sidekick's easygoing passivity—grows impatient with what is really weakness and neediness.

Given time, most sidekicks will begin to feel trapped, trampled on, and powerless in their role. What was once a safe haven from the world has become a dank and depressing prison. They might say: "I wish I were dead," or "I wish I could just go to sleep and not wake up." **Note: If you can identify with either of these statements, please seek counseling right away. No one deserves to feel that kind of pain and isolation.**

Just like the superstar, the sidekick sees things mostly in black and white. Any criticism of him equals rejection and condemnation. The difference comes in the way he processes negative responses. While the superstar deflects blame, the sidekick publicly will take blame and condemn himself.

Sidekicks often see themselves in terms of "human doings" rather than "human beings." Whenever a person gains his or her sense of personal value from what he or she *does* instead of who he or she *is,* that person can look forward to a life without boundaries. People line up to take advantage of those lacking the backbone to say "NO."

In marriage, sidekicks often say "yes" when they really mean "no." They're stopped by a little voice that whispers, "You don't have the right to say no, or you'll be bad!" As a result, sidekicks are forever getting trampled on and taken advantage of by others.

THE SCAPEGOAT

"The scapegoat" is the unwitting villain (or victim) in our dysfunctional cast of characters. Most family scapegoats are either a middle child or last child.

In the Old Testament, the term "scapegoat" literally meant the sacrifice of a goat during the rite of atonement. Today, scapegoats are found in every arena, from political scandals to the baseball player who strikes out with the bases loaded, to marriages that end in divorce. In dysfunctional families, scapegoats serve as human shields, bearing the brunt of the anger, tension, and frustrations from the others.

Instead of being sacrificed as a sin offering, modern scapegoats are subject to the fate of becoming defeatists. Raised to feel inferior to their siblings, scapegoats seem to believe that low self-esteem and negative thinking is a normal way of life.

Like every character in our script, scapegoats usually repeat their role in married life. They invariably select controlling, perfectionist, superstar mates who are only too happy to blame them for any mistakes.

While scapegoats are accustomed to taking the blame when things go wrong, they may eventually grow tired of being a human doormat. Despite this growing resentment, they are often unable to effect positive changes in their lives. The sense of powerlessness over those around them they felt as children has shadowed them through adolescence and adulthood. Sadly, when scapegoats divorce and remarry, they often find themselves trapped in the same pattern again.

Since any flicker of emotional maturity was quickly extinguished within the family system, the majority of adult scapegoats suffer from intense insecurities. Allowing a child scapegoat to break free from this role and mature normally would mean affording them a sense of self-reliance and power. In dysfunctional family units, the other cast members couldn't allow that, not if they want to keep their little scapegoat penned up and available for service. They also secretly fear being cast into this role should the real scapegoat stop playing his part.

"Scapegoats aren't worthy of a better life." That's their childhood script, and they stick to it, not because it feels good to take blame, but because it's a role they completely understand. Habits, even destructive ones, are hard to break.

Adult scapegoats are classically passive-aggressive. Like the sidekick, they say yes when they plan to say no. For example, she might "accidentally" burn a hole in her husband's shirt while ironing, and then apologize profusely. Or he might forget to run an important errand that his superstar wife warned *had* to be done.

Do you fit this role? If you aren't sure whether you fit into the scapegoat role, answer the following three questions:

1. *Who has the power in your marriage?*

2. *Do you feel more like a mature adult or a frightened, insecure child?*

3. *Have you learned how to set boundaries for your spouse? (If your answer is no, you'll find the chapter on boundaries particularly interesting.)*

In marriage, as in childhood, adult scapegoats constantly fret over separation and abandonment. This fear often takes the form of unfounded jealousy or wild accusations of infidelity, both of which drive a wedge into relationships. Ironically, the very thing scapegoats fear the most—being alone—is often the final outcome of their intolerable behavior.

THE FORGOTTEN CHILD

"The Forgotten Child" is a bit player in the dysfunctional family cast. This person shows up day after day hoping to get into a scene, only to leave empty handed. He may land an occasional bit part, but nothing of substance. He craves bigger roles and more recognition, but eventually decides there's no point in trying. Even when he gets into a scene, the part invariably ends up on the cutting room floor.

In the hit comedy movie "Home Alone," the lead character, Kevin, plays a classic forgotten child. His extended family is so large that he clearly assumes a middle child position, although he's actually the youngest. Lost within the family system, he's accidentally left at home as everybody leaves on vacation.

Forgotten children don't feel as important as their older siblings or as cute and helpless as their younger brothers and sisters. Consequently, they often wind up searching outside the family unit for the acceptance and identity they so desperately need. They deal with the tension of their place in life by emotionally distancing themselves from the family to escape into their own little world.

Even when a forgotten child marries, those old feelings of isolation and obscurity are waiting to pounce. Forgotten types allow their spouses to move just so close emotionally before pulling away out of fear of rejection. Unfortunately, it's that very fear that usually ends up "gumming up" the marital works.

If you play this role in your marriage, you may have a subconscious "trap door wish," an escape clause that allows you to escape from intimate, mature relationships before getting too close emotionally. Ironically, you're desperate for that closeness, and that causes you tremendous inner turmoil.

A forgotten child has difficulty accepting compliments. Acceptance, or recognition, forces him out of hiding and into a relationship. He dreads making presentations to bosses and coworkers. He's far more comfortable working independently than in groups. His motto in life is "Stay camouflaged" or "Blend in."

If you think your forgotten child is still active in your life, the first step for you is to find safe relationships. If your spouse has the capacity to empathize with your feelings of loneliness and isolation, share those feelings with him or her. If you question your mate's ability to empathize with your pain, your next move may be to join a support group or seek counseling. As long as you continue to feel forgotten and ignored, you will remain in that role. Once you begin discussing your needs—ideally with your spouse, a close friend, or in therapy—you'll understand their legitimacy.

THE VICTIM ROLE

Remember those old Shirley Temple movies? Between the singing and tap-dancing, poor little Shirley was orphaned, homeless, ridiculed, or hungry. She was a victim. In real life, however, the "victim's" role is usually cast by controlling family members. Victims can turn up anywhere in the birth sequence, but they are most often the first or last born.

Often saddled with dysfunctional parents, adult victims can struggle with feelings of helplessness and unworthiness for a lifetime.

Victims don't see a cup as half empty or half full. To them, it's too obscured by water spots and cracks to see what's inside. They view God as being a million miles away, certainly too remote to answer their prayers. They have trouble with the concept of a loving, personal God. They're often overheard mumbling things such as, "If it weren't for bad luck, I wouldn't have any luck at all."

Victims commonly rebuff compliments. Tell them they did a great job and they'll deflect the praise. That is because they've lived a lifetime of viewing themselves as unworthy and powerless to change anything. Compliments suggest they may indeed have some power and control over their lives, a mystifying and frightening concept for victims. Despite their unhappiness, it's much easier and safer to live the "status quo" (victimized and powerless), rather than acknowledge any growth potential.

Victims believe they're just destined to fail. New people in their lives only represent new chances to be hurt. A new job is a chance to be fired. A new car is probably a lemon. A marriage will lead to a divorce. The victim's attitude is, "Don't expect anything and you won't be disappointed."

Victims routinely set themselves up for failure and disappointment. They set a trap for themselves, then fall into it. Let's say, for example, that a victim is honored with an award. Although he secretly hopes family and friends will attend, he says, "It's no big deal. You don't need to show up." Of course, when nobody shows, the victim feels hurt, rejected, and angry.

Like a silent movie heroine tied to the railroad tracks, the victim prays to be swept up and carried to safety by a handsome stranger. The hero may save the day, but he finds it impossible to save the victim from her own unhappiness and is driven away. No problem. Victims are good at recruiting new heroes.

Victims are seldom happy. When the cycle of disappointment comes full circle—as it inevitably does—they're disappointed once again. They may even pray for God to take their lives and end their pain and suffering. They reach bottom and decide it's too late to recruit a rescuer. They wouldn't mind if God did end it for them.

Since victims usually expect the worst, they're in a continuous state of high anxiety. This way of thinking can result in a myriad of emotional problems, including but not limited to the following:

- sleeplessness
- phobias (unnatural fears)
- obsessive thoughts (constant concern of something bad happening)
- compulsive behaviors (shopping, spending, cleaning)
- panic attacks (fear of dying, hyperventilating, chest pains, shortness of breath, dizziness).

Victims classically feel alone and misunderstood in their marriages. That is because their way of thinking causes them to feel helpless. Victims must begin to see themselves as significant and worthy before they can make their needs known. Like the forgotten child, the first step out of character for the victim may be to seek counseling or support groups. The victim needs to practice communicating his or her needs in a safe environment, without fear of further rejection.

THE COMIC KID

Within every clown, they say, beats the heart of a sad, lonely child. In my profession, I've mostly found this to be true. "The Comedian" assumes a lighthearted veneer to protect himself from outside pain and pressures. As a child, he uses humor as a defense mechanism for dealing with critical, angry, or abusive parents. It also enables him to wrestle a little attention away from the superstars, scapegoats, and victims of the dysfunctional family system.

As adults, comedians continue to avoid their own needs—and those of their spouses—by making light of or minimizing serious situations. For example, a wife might complain about an upsetting incident on the job. The comedian husband answers his wife with a joke. The wife might find this amusing at first, but ultimately this behavior leads to an emotional split in the relationship, with the comedian's mate feeling cast off and alone. Certainly, she doesn't feel as though she can trust her mate with any serious issues.

Ironically, the comedian expects to have his needs met, despite doing absolutely nothing to communicate them. He desperately seeks love and acceptance, but without a clue of how to achieve it from his mate. The jovial facade and penchant for minimizing serious problems doesn't help matters. In the end, both partners are feeling very much alone in their marriage.

WHAT'S NEXT?

If you're feeling alone in your marriage, the role you played as a child could be part of the problem. If you haven't already done so, take time to discover how the characters in your family system interacted. How did you fit in? And have you repeated the same role in your adult life? If so, now is the time to break out of the mold!

Once you have identified your role, it's useful to determine what role your spouse played in his or her family. Certain cast members seem to attract other cast members. For instance, if you have identified yourself as a scapegoat, chances are you're married to a superstar.

The following questions will help guide your thinking:

1. *Did your family system pressure you into your childhood role? If so, how?*

2. *What role if any did your spouse play in his or her family during childhood?*

3. *How did your family script shape your childhood, adolescence, and adult years? Though the cast members have changed, has your role remained the same?*

4. *Ask yourself if your childhood role served you well throughout your adult years. If your answer is "NO," then commit to change.*

5. *How does your childhood role create conflicts in your marriage?*

HOW CAN I CHANGE MY ROLE?

If you feel that the role you have been playing has contributed to your feelings of isolation and aloneness in your marriage, there are several things that might help you begin the change process. Start writing a daily journal. On the first page, write down the characteristics of your role. When you find yourself slipping into a destructive characteristic, jot down the date, the time, and the circumstance. Make a note of whom you were talking to, what was going through your mind, and how the situation was or wasn't resolved. Additionally, ask yourself if you are dealing with the problem or situation as an adult or are still trapped in your childhood role.

After a few weeks, you'll begin to recognize what triggers your dependency on a role. Remember that you have power to break the pattern. Over time, spotting those triggers will be second nature. You'll learn to deal with potentially problematic situations in a positive way.

For example, victims retreat when they sense anger. They feel powerless to change or to assert their needs. In order for change to occur, victims must view anger differently. Instead of feeling as though they're bad, as a result of somebody else's anger, they must view that anger as being out of their control—somebody else's problem. Once they stop trying to take responsibility for what isn't theirs, they will realize there are behavior choices.

HOLLY'S HAPPY ENDING

After several counseling sessions, Holly's view of herself and her husband gradually changed. She now understood how her role as a childhood superstar—always being the responsible and mature person—had impaired her adult relationships, especially her marriage.

"It's amazing," she laughed. "A month ago I was certain divorce was inevitable. To tell you the truth, I only made an appointment with you as a technicality. It was my way of absolving myself from any guilt whatsoever.

"Anyway, now I understand why my husband was never around. I was a royal pain," she said. "Sure, I was unhappy and lonely, but that's exactly how he felt around me. And I told him so."

I explained to Holly that it would take time—with a few bumps along the way—before she fully divested herself of her childhood role. I also told her that being honest with her husband put her on the fast track to a happier marriage.

"It's amazing, the change I've seen in John," she added, enthusiastically. "He's more attentive and more interested in including me in his activities. He's even considering starting his own promotional gift business at home, so we can spend more time with our daughter."

It's never easy to learn to play a different role or to drop negative roles. Why should it be? We've played our old roles all of our lives! Even with heightened insight, it's easy to slip into our roles from the past from time to time. Your job is to give these scene-stealers a quick "hook" before they damage the progress you have made in your marriage.

CHAPTER FOUR

The Freedom
of Forgiveness

Let bygones be bygones. Forgive and forget. Laudable senti-
ments to be sure. But let's be practical: To err is human, to
forgive is downright unusual, especially in a troubled marriage.

Some husbands and wives become so immersed in their own
feelings of anger, blame, resentment, and revenge that positive
emotions are shelved indefinitely. The basics of a loving relationship, such as empathy, become distant memories for some
couples. Both people strap on their pain like a loaded revolver,
poised and ready to unload on the nearest target—usually an
unsuspecting spouse.

Is there a hair-trigger in your family? A compassion-impaired
partner who keeps throwing past failures back in your face? Or
are you the one doing the mudslinging? Either way, such behavior will invariably result in your feeling alone in your marriage.

Do you ever go to bed irate with your mate only to wake up
seething? Have you given the devil not only a foothold into
your marriage but convenient grab handles as well? Paul wrote
in Ephesians 4:26-27 (Living Bible), "If you are angry, don't sin
by nursing your grudge. Don't let the sun go down when you
are still angry—get over it quickly; for while you are angry you
give a mighty foothold to the devil."

Are you guilty of serving up a steady diet of reheated grief over something that happened last week, last month, or twenty years ago? Or are you on the receiving end of these attacks? It could have been a careless remark about your mother-in-law or an ill-advised comment about dress size. It might have been a disappointment, an embarrassment, or an affair that keeps raising its ugly head.

The late actress Marlene Dietrich placed this lighthearted but useful spin on forgiveness: "Once you forgive your man, don't warm up his sins for breakfast."

THE TOXIC SNOWBALL EFFECT

After thirty-five years of marriage, Mary and Bob were in agreement on few things. But they did agree that the last fifteen years of their marriage had been less than fulfilling. On a hopeful note, they also agreed to seek counseling.

It was clear from the outset that a string of small problems and irritants had piled up in their marriage like dust atop a refrigerator. Left unresolved, these issues grew, causing what I call "The Toxic Snowball Effect."

As the name implies, the Toxic Snowball Effect starts with a series of seemingly small hurts that gain momentum and intensity over the years. The larger the snowball grows, the more isolated, angry, and alone people feel in their marriages.

Bob's penchant for flirting got the snowball rolling in his and Mary's marriage. "He flirts at church, at parties, the supermarket. He even flirts while waiting at a red light," Mary complained during our first session. "If I can't find him, you can bet he's talking to some woman. Doesn't he care how that makes me feel?"

Throughout most of their marriage, Mary kept her feelings of belittlement and anger hidden from her husband. Instead of telling her husband how she felt, she'd punish him with quick personal jabs or by withholding sexual intimacy or by investing all of her time in outside activities.

Bob, not exactly a master at sensitivity, was nonetheless aware of his wife's nonverbalized feelings. Still, he persisted in the behavior in order to strike back and get her attention. "I wasn't flirting," he said. "It's not my fault women enjoy talking to me. What should I do, come running over and ask your permission first?"

Mary's hurt and anger only fueled Bob's defensiveness and resentment. "If you'd care a little more about my needs, maybe I wouldn't need to talk to other women!" he said during a typical flareup. What had started as a tiny puff of snow was now on the verge of wiping out an entire marriage.

Every toxic snowball consists of the following easy-to-find ingredients: resentment, immaturity, poor communication, fear, and blame.

Let's take a look at these ingredients.

Insensitivity. It doesn't take a Ph.D. to understand that insensitivity creates difficulties in a marriage. The best marriages feature two people continually striving to understand each other's concerns and needs and doing their best to meet those needs. Our mission is to help you pursue ways of improving your marriage, despite your insensitive spouse.

Resentment. Resentment crept into Bob and Mary's marriage under the cover of mutually unresolved anger. Bob saw himself as dead last on his wife's priority list—somewhere behind church, friends, kids, and the family dog. Instead of openly addressing his needs, he gave in to resentment. Flirting became a surefire way of getting his wife's attention. Mary had her share of unprocessed anger and disappointments as well. Again, instead of communicating her feelings, she punished Bob by withholding companionship and love.

Immaturity. Maturity, to a large degree, can be measured by the ability to convey normal adult needs. Had Bob and Mary been mature enough, they would have vocalized their painful and angry feelings. They would have clearly labeled their needs and sought out opportunities to meet them. Instead, they punished one another emotionally.

Poor communication. Had they possessed good communication skills, Bob and Mary could have avoided many of their problems. Bob could have reinforced his love for Mary, and conveyed the value he placed on their time together. Mary could have been forthright about her fears and resentments, and discussed openly her feelings about his flirting. The snowball would have been stopped in its tracks, and the groundwork would have been laid for a positive resolution to their difficulties.

Fear. People react differently to fear. Some grab their rifles, mount their bayonets, and charge up the hill. Others hunker down defensively in their foxholes. Undoubtedly, fear is at the very core of our "fight-or-flight" nature. It can lead us to lash out in anger or retreat. Whatever the response, the motive remains the same: self-preservation at all costs—even at the cost of a marriage.

Bob and Mary could have avoided years of pain by communicating their fears. In Bob's case, it was the fear of becoming less important to his wife and that intimacy was waning. Most of all, Bob feared REJECTION! Similarly, Mary could have communicated her fear of abandonment and her fear of being compared and not measuring up to other women. She could have communicated her fear that intimacy was waning. Most of all, Mary feared REJECTION!

It's no coincidence that Bob and Mary shared the same basic fears. All of us do.

Blame. There's always plenty of blame to go around within troubled marriages. However, blame is a matter of choice, not an entitlement. Choose to blame and you are choosing to stay angry. Choose to blame and you will never take responsibility for healing the pain. Choose to blame, and you had better get used to feeling alone.

When it comes to blame, we're behind the wheel. We've got control. If you were married to someone who was unfaithful, whose fault would that be? Arguably, not yours. But your happiness is still your responsibility. If you neglect what falls within your control, you're shirking your responsibility. You're surrendering to anger and choosing to live your life buried in blame.

THE "UPSET OF THE MONTH CLUB"

There ought to be an organization for people who hang on to the past, a club where empathy is discouraged, sympathy is suspect, and forgiveness is forbidden. We could call it the "Upset of the Month Club." Advertisements might be worded along these lines:

Attention, Professional Victims!

Running out of old upsets and hurts? Been too long since your spouse wronged you? Join the "Upset of the Month Club," and suffer to your heart's content! Become a member and receive your first tirade absolutely free! After that, receive one major upset or outburst (your choice) each and every month.

Keep only the painful memories you can use—attacks, rejections, broken promises—and send back the rest. Remember, you're under no obligation. Act now, and we'll rush you these whiny, all-time classic hits:

Yakity Yak... Don't Talk Back
Heartbreak Hotel
Your Cheatin' Heart
Tears on My Pillow
You Talk Too Much
Mother-in-Law

You will also receive other painful classics of the 60s, 70s, and 80s absolutely free. Plus, you'll automatically receive our monthly newsletter jam-packed with articles and tips, including:

- Forgiving is for fools
- Dredging up the derbies hypnosis missed
- How to hold a grudge 'til the day you die
- How to connect your car's battery to his oatmeal spoon

Join today, and start torturing your spouse tomorrow! Think how miserable they'll be!

Did you get your order in? Good. Remember, it takes six to eight weeks for delivery, and while you're waiting, why not give forgiveness a try! It's the best investment you will ever make!

FORGIVENESS ISN'T AN OPTION

One of the reasons you may be experiencing loneliness in your marriage is that you are trapped in feelings of resentment, anger, and unforgiveness toward your mate. At this point, you have a choice: You can either stay stuck in your unhappiness, or you can move toward forgiveness and a better relationship with your spouse.

There are many options in life for Christians, but forgiveness isn't one of them. Thankfully, the Bible left us with an amazing, uplifting, and powerful paper trail on forgiveness. The subject is discussed no less than seventy-five times in the Bible, including the following passage.

Paul wrote a letter to the church in Rome to introduce himself and share his message of love, grace, and forgiveness prior to his arrival. "Do not repay anyone evil for evil. Be careful to do what is right in the eyes of everybody. If it is possible, as far as it depends on you, live at peace with everyone. Do not take revenge, my friends, but leave room for God's wrath, for it is written: 'It is mine to avenge; I will repay,' says the Lord" (Rom 12:17-19).

I find that many who are unhappy in their marriages are

actively repaying evil with evil. As Paul has shown, this is clearly not God's word.

One of my favorite illustrations of forgiveness in Scripture is found in Luke 7:37-47. Jesus was dealing with Simon the Pharisee, an arrogant legalist.

Simon, aware that growing crowds of people were following Jesus, decided to invite the new celebrity to his home for lunch. Shortly after, a prostitute arrived at the house with gifts for Jesus. Once inside, "as she stood behind him at his feet weeping, she began to wet his feet with her tears. Then she wiped them with her hair, kissed them, and poured perfume on them" (Lk 7:37-38).

Simon was outraged. If Jesus was really so holy, he reasoned, how could he possibly allow a common whore to get so close, much less wash his feet! Jesus intercepted his thoughts and told Simon the story of two debtors.

"Two men owed money to a certain moneylender. One owed him five hundred denarii, and the other fifty. Neither of them had the money to pay him back, so he canceled the debts of both. Now which of them will love him more?" (Lk 7:41-42).

Simon answered correctly—the debtor who owed more to the moneylender.

Jesus pointed out that the prostitute, who realized she was spiritually bankrupt, was grateful to be in his presence and she had a deep desire to be cleansed and forgiven.

"You did not give me a kiss, but this woman, from the time I entered, has not stopped kissing my feet. You did not put oil on my head, but she has poured perfume on my feet. Therefore, I tell you, her many sins have been forgiven—for she loved much. But he who has been forgiven little loves little" (Lk 7:45-47).

Jesus' message reminds us not to be so self-righteous, so positive that we are 100 percent right, that we refuse to reach out for forgiveness. I've known people who would rather be miserable and alone in their marriages than ask their spouse for forgiveness.

WHY DO PEOPLE REFUSE TO FORGIVE?

Some people refuse to forgive simply to ensure their position as a victim. In refusing to forgive, an individual often views his or her marital problems as the latest in a long line of life's cruel blows. "Isn't this typical of my life?" they think.

Some refuse to forgive because the act of forgiveness would force them to see themselves from a different perspective, making them accountable for their own happiness.

While some people simply refuse to forgive, others maintain a sort of power over their spouse by zinging their mate with past pains or dangling forgiveness just out of reach. They punish their mates by keeping them off balance and fearful.

When the polls close, and the votes are tallied, people who refuse to forgive are the losers on two counts: (1) They're still unhappy and feeling alone, and (2) they've fallen away from God's word by withholding forgiveness. Remember, forgiveness not only benefits you, it's the right thing to do!

FORGIVENESS: A PROCESS

No, forgiveness isn't always an easy process, especially when we're provoked or pushed to our limits. Even the apostles had their difficulties with the subject.

Here's what Christ instructed them: "Rebuke your brother if he sins, and forgive him if he is sorry. Even if he wrongs you seven times a day and each time turns again and asks forgiveness, forgive him" (Lk 17:4, Living Bible).

The apostles must have been thinking, "Sure, that's easy for you to say—you're the Lord. As for us, we need more faith; tell us how to get it" (see Luke 17:5).

Jesus describes a laborer who has just finished his assigned tasks for the day: "Would [you] thank the servant because he did what he was told to do? So you also, when you have done everything you were told to do, should say, 'We are unworthy servants; we have only done our duty'" (Lk 17:9-10).

Forgiveness is the cornerstone of our faith, part of our job description as Christians. Our willingness to forgive should be as strong as our desire to be forgiven. When we open our hearts and forgive, we are only doing our duty as children of God.

However, when you're feeling alone in your marriage, the ability to forgive can help open that window of opportunity toward understanding and meaningful communication with your spouse. Nothing breaks the emotional gridlock in a relationship like a little forgiveness. Let's face it, even if your spouse is the one inflicting most of the pain, you must have inflicted some pain somewhere.

WHAT IS FORGIVENESS?

Can you imagine how our lives would be without God's grace and desire to forgive us? We would be in sorry shape, to be sure. But before attempting to apply his message of forgiveness in your marriage, let's look at some myths about forgiveness.

Giving credit where credit is due, some of these myths and their corresponding truths were first developed by my friend and colleague, Dr. John Townsend of the Minirth-Meier Clinic West.

Myth: Forgiving means forgetting.
Truth: When we forget, we invite more pain. Scripture doesn't instruct us to forget hurtful acts. On the contrary, we are told in Matthew 10:16 to be as "shrewd as snakes and as innocent as doves" in our human relationships.

For example, let's say you stop by the automatic teller machine late one evening. On your way back to your car, two thugs spring from behind the bushes and take your money. Forgiveness for the two men is certainly possible, but would you really want to forget the lesson you learned about late-night

ATM withdrawals? Hopefully, you would learn some caution from that experience.

Forgetting closes our eyes to the truth and leaves us vulnerable to further pain. While it's prudent to be cautious, always maintain your capacity for forgiveness and peacemaking.

For instance, in a marriage where one spouse has had an affair, it is imperative that he or she work toward forgiveness and toward trying to restore trust. Trying to forget immediately creates too much insecurity, since that foundation of trust has yet to be reestablished. Forgetting is a natural byproduct of forgiveness, coupled with the passage of time.

Myth: Forgiveness means acquittal.
Truth: When we acquit, we are saying the sin never happened. Acting as though the sin didn't happen is denial at its worst. If you're angry, be angry. If you're hurt, be hurt. Before you can forgive, you must first acknowledge that you have been sinned against. Many of us stop short of that acknowledgement out of anger, anxiety, or fear.

Departing from denial enables you to identify your injury and better understand the origin of its pain. Remember, problems arise in relationships when we deny our emotions and fail to understand why we feel the way we do.

Myth: Forgiveness is a decision.
Truth: Forgiveness is a process. Couples and therapists often make the error of racing too quickly toward forgiveness in marriage counseling. But lasting forgiveness can't be switched on and off. Only after you've made a thoughtful decision to enter the loop of forgiveness will the process actually begin.

Myth: Forgiveness means reconciliation.
Truth: Forgiving may lead to reconciliation. Reconciliation takes two people. A good biblical example is found in Matthew 18:21-22: "Then Peter came to Jesus and asked, 'Lord, how many times shall I forgive my brother when he sins against me? Up to seven times?'

"Jesus answered, 'I tell you, not seven times, but seventy times seven.'"

Some people simply aren't interested in reconciliation. Sometimes this is simply the result of a heart that has hardened. At some point, love ceases to be unconditional and becomes an invitation to more emotional pain.

When you've fully communicated your feelings—given the other person every opportunity to make amends and nothing changes—it's time to back off and protect yourself from further emotional pain. You may need to put reconciliation on hold until your spouse is ready to make changes.

Myth: The sinner must ask for forgiveness.
Truth: The sinner need not acknowledge the deed. Few people are mature enough to seek forgiveness. Does this mean we're supposed to wait patiently for a remnant of repentance or a morsel of remorse? No way! What happens if someone dies before he or she asks for forgiveness? Is it a lost opportunity or a missed chance to be free of the resentment? Hardly!

Fortunately, we can free ourselves from resentment by forgiving. The other person doesn't have to be present, willing, or even living in order for us to forgive. Here's one technique I employ in therapy: I ask my patient to try to empathize with the person he or she is considering forgiving. This allows him or her to understand that person's shortcomings, failings, and human frailties that may have contributed to the objectionable behavior. For example, you may recognize the effects of childhood problems that contributed to someone's role as a victimizer. Once you gain an overhead perspective of his or her life, you stand a better chance of understanding the choices the person makes.

Myth: I can make him or her repent.
Truth: You can't make him or her do anything. Some of us think that lording forgiveness over an individual will prevent him or her from hurting us again and drive that person to

repentance. But we're powerless on both counts, and the sooner we understand that the better. The only control we have is over our own forgiveness.

Myth: If I withhold forgiveness, I've got the upper hand.
Truth: Controlling and manipulating never gives you the upper hand. Withholding forgiveness may be a tempting thought, but it never achieves the desired effect of driving another person into submission. After we've been emotionally injured, we're in a weakened and highly vulnerable position. When the offender shows the slightest shred of remorse, we often seize it as a down payment. We're finally in the driver's seat for a change, and it feels pretty good.

That power vanishes, however, when the other person grows tired of the game. Nobody appreciates having something lorded over them. At some point resentment gathers steam and turns toxic. Before long, the sinner decides there's no longer any point in saying "I'm sorry."

Myth: Once a sinner, always a sinner.
Truth: We're all sinners, but people do change. If there was one central theme in the Bible, it would be: "I'm not OK. You're not OK. But we can be OK with God." The truth is that we are all sinners. Fortunately for us, God understands and allows us grace. With that in mind, shouldn't you give your spouse the opportunity to change—without withholding your forgiveness?

Myth: Forgiveness is for the sinner.
Truth: Forgiveness is for you, not the sinner. Perhaps the biggest myth about forgiveness is that it takes the sinner off the hook. It doesn't. It does, however, release *you* from your scriptural responsibility to forgive. Not only that, it frees you from resentment and all sorts of negative emotions associated with unforgiveness. God tells us to forgive partly because it purifies our hearts.

THE COST OF UNFORGIVENESS

You have the choice whether to forgive or whether to hold on to your anger and bitterness. We've already discussed why you should forgive, even when the person who hurt you is unrepentant. What if you choose not to forgive? What if what that person has done is just too much for you to let go of?

When we choose to withhold forgiveness, we're choosing to hold on to ugly and harmful emotions and actions. Harboring a grudge and refusing to forgive takes its toll on us, both emotionally and physically. If these emotions aren't properly dealt with there can be disastrous consequences. Refusing to forgive opens us up to many emotional and psychological ailments. Here are some emotional problems commonly seen in people who withhold forgiveness:

- Chronic depression
- Anxiety disorders (stress and tension)
- Anger and resentment
- Chronic unhappiness
- Fatigue
- Sleep-related disorders, including insomnia (trouble getting to sleep or staying asleep), hypersomnia (sleeping too much) and frequent nightmares (the mind's way of releasing anxiety)
- Vindictiveness, which is a conscious or subconscious desire to seek revenge and to hurt others in retaliation for your hurts
- Codependency, which is giving up your sense of who you are and taking responsibility for another's feelings and happiness
- Victim mentality, which is a pervasive sense that you will never get what you need to be happy and that others always take advantage of you

Physical ailments that can come from withholding forgiveness can include:

- Ulcers
- Gastrointestinal problems
- Nervous stomach
- Irritable bowel syndrome
- Headaches (including migraines)

Hopefully, I've convinced you that forgiveness is not only the key to moving forward in your marriage, but an absolute necessity for living a happy, healthy life.

LEARNING TO FORGIVE

Forgiveness requires plenty of emotional stoop labor, but considering the alternative—a marriage of isolation and loneliness—it's well worth your effort.

Perhaps at this point you're thinking, "I know I'd be better off if I could forgive. I know that God wants me to forgive. But it's not that simple. Besides, the last time I tried to forgive my spouse and made myself vulnerable, it blew up in my face. I was very hurt. I won't be a fool and forgive him again."

Or perhaps you've tried to make changes in yourself. Maybe you've seen a therapist or talked to your pastor and close friends. You've pored over pertinent passages in the Bible and found nothing that seems to apply to you. You're still angry at the world and, most of all, your mate. Well, there's probably too much distance between anger and forgiveness in your relationship. Just as labor negotiations must proceed point by point in order to close the gap between union and management, forgiveness must be approached in an orderly fashion in your marriage.

So stay on the following stepping stones to forgiveness. Jumping off before you reach the final stone only heightens your chances of becoming more hurt and angry, and having to start all over again.

Examine your past. Examining your past has practical applications to marriage repair. Here are a few questions you or your spouse can look at to help you determine if you came from a childhood where forgiveness and grace were rare commodities.

1. Did love feel conditional as you were growing up?

2. When you did something wrong or bad, did it feel as if you were out of your parents' good graces for a period of time?

3. Can you look back and see a pattern of withdrawing or hiding from your parents when you did something that they didn't approve of?

4. Did it seem as if your parents didn't love you as much for a time after you really messed up?

5. Did you get compared with a sibling and often feel like you didn't measure up?

6. Did you feel like your parents hated you, instead of what you did whe n you did something bad?

7. When your parents argued, did it usually take a long time for them to make up?

8. Do you recall your parents never asking you to forgive them for something they did wrong?

9. Do you recall your parents never asking each other for forgiveness?

10. Did one or both of your parents hold on to their anger and make it obvious to everyone in the house that they were angry?

If you answered most of these questions "yes," then you may have learned improper techniques for handling forgiveness.

Remember, we learn best by example. If your parents understood the concept of grace and forgiveness, then you're probably fairly strong in that area. If they were deficient in that area, you are likely to be deficient as well. But you need to be careful not to blame your parents. Their responsibility to teach these lessons ended when you become an adult. Now it's your responsibility.

Break out of denial. We stay in denial for two reasons: to avoid dealing with past pain and to avoid being hurt in the future.

Many marital problems are a result of a series of emotional hurts buried in denial. In order to uncap denial and enter forgiveness you must:

1. *Acknowledge that an emotional injury has taken place and that you have been hurt.*
2. *Identify the emotional injury and begin to understand why and how it happened.*
3. *Commit to bringing and leaving the injury in the light so that it can be addressed and worked through.*

Remember, God never denies that our sins or hurts happened. But he always provides a solution if we are willing to be open and honest about them.

Assume responsibility, not blame. The main objective of counseling is to help people focus on those things that fall within their control. In other words, if you view your spouse as the person who is making you feel alone and unhappy, you're looking in the wrong direction. If you've been waiting for your spouse to beg for forgiveness, for example, you may be in for a long wait.

Taking responsibility means taking the initiative to improve your situation. Blame causes you to remain in a stagnant position while waiting for others to take action.

In counseling, a pivotal concept is learning to deal with what is "ours" and allowing others to deal with what is "theirs." For instance, I counseled one couple who argued constantly over finances, to the point where the marriage nearly collapsed. She blamed him for not working enough overtime. If he worked more, she reasoned, he'd bring home more money, thus easing their financial burdens. She viewed his lack of income as a lack of commitment to her. She never considered, however, taking a part-time job or learning how to establish a family budget.

She finally understood that she wasn't powerless in this situation. She could help ease the financial strain, which she did. She chose to take a part-time job and enroll in a family budgeting class at her local community college. The moment she began facing up to her part of the problem, her husband decided to accept some overtime at work.

Understand your anger. Anger encompasses a full range of feelings, from mild disappointment to intense disgust and hatred. Turned outward, anger alienates and distances you from others. Turned inward, it can lead to a slow, painful emotional death.

And let's not forget anger's ugly first cousin: revenge. When we're weighted down in an unforgiving, vengeful state of mind, we're powerless to progress. We spend our time thinking of ways to get even. What a waste! Remove anger, and you remove the need to seek revenge.

Here are a few tips in dealing with anger:

1. *Identify the source of the anger.*
2. *Experience your anger by releasing it appropriately. You accom - plish this by "talking through" your anger, ideally with your spouse, rather than complaining or letting the pain build with - in.*
3. *Grieve what needs to be grieved.* Grieving allows us to process painful emotions. When angry or painful emotions are addressed, they usually diminish in power and intensity. Grieving is commonly associated with sadness, such as the death of a loved one. However, we also grieve over lost expectations, such as those in a lonely, failing marriage. It's always healthy to examine your losses and grieve over them. This is a process that begins with understanding your expec- tations. Maybe you thought you'd be happier at this point in your relationship. You thought your spouse would be more attentive to your needs. Whatever the situation, grieving any loss will allow you to deal with the reality of your circum- stances without anguishing over every crashed expectation.

It's perfectly OK to experience sadness and shed tears if

necessary. Be cautious, though, not to allow your grieving to turn to self-pity. Grieving allows you to release the old and take constructive steps toward a better future. Some couples, for example, grieve over the fact that they are unable to have children. This allows them to experience the sadness and move forward. In this case, moving forward could mean adopting or looking into alternative fertilization methods. Whatever the answer, grieving is a permanent process. I can't tell you when it's time to stop grieving, only that you need to stop and move on at some point.

4. *Take the necessary steps to ensure this particular hurt doesn't happen again.* If you are constantly placing yourself in situations where you are being taken advantage of, ask yourself: why? What is it about *you* that keeps you in an emotionally vulnerable position? Are you slipping back into a victim's role?

5. *Take personal responsibility for forgiving and moving past the anger.* It's always healthy to step back and ask yourself, "What am I really angry about, or with whom? Is this person really guilty?" Many people find their anger is rooted in old emotional injuries or childhood events carted off as "baggage" into adulthood. Discarding this baggage may be the best thing you've ever done for your marriage.

Don't isolate yourself. If you're interested in working toward forgiveness—and resolving conflicts—you have two basic options: You can either hide in your pain or you can bring your pain into the open, thus dealing with it. You probably have already realized that isolation provides only brief protection from pain. True, temporary withdrawal to gather your thoughts may be helpful at times, but remaining isolated only leads to worse problems, such as depression.

Working through hurts and toward forgiveness is easier by not attempting to do it alone. I've yet to find a Bible passage that advises us to hide in our closets until all is forgiven.

The forgiveness process is accelerated when you connect with others. This may mean a pastor, friend, or counselor. Whoever it is, you must have support and a person to help you process feelings.

IF ALL ELSE FAILS

If after going through these steps, you still feel unable to forgive, prayerfully think about the following:

1. *Do I really want to forgive, or am I using my anger and unforgiveness as a weapon against my spouse?*

2. *What is there to fear if I were to let go of my anger and begin to forgive?*

3. *Do I really want to repair my marriage badly enough to let go of my anger and begin to forgive?*

4. *Have my anger and lack of forgiveness served me well?*

5. *Have my anger and unforgiveness made me a happier person?*

6. *Do I feel more lost and alone now than ever before?*

7. *Am I willing to stop focusing on my spouse and allow change in myself?*

What do you want your next step to be? Do you want to continue in your anger, miserable and unable to relate to your spouse? Or do you want to move into a forgiving, loving relationship with that person? The choice is yours!

LOVE IS A DECISION

We have the power to change ourselves and begin loving again by setting a new behavioral course. It's simply a matter of motivation and knowing where to begin.

Where is forgiveness on your own priority list? There's no doubt that your inability—or unwillingness—to forgive can become the single biggest obstacle standing between you and a happy relationship for you and your spouse.

Paul writes: "Let all bitterness, wrath, anger, clamor, and evil speaking be put away from you with all malice. And be kind to one another, tenderhearted, forgiving one another, just as God in Christ forgave you" (Eph 4:31-32, Living Bible).

As I've said before, the choice to forgive and walk in love is completely yours. God isn't going to force you to forgive your spouse. But it's also not his will that you go through life miserable and unable to love your spouse. Whatever it takes, make forgiveness a priority in your marriage and in the rest of your life!

CHAPTER FIVE

Overcoming Expectations

Just about anybody involved in an unhappy marriage can look back and see that this wasn't what they expected when they got married. Expectations are a part of any relationship, including marriage. But expectations that are inflated or unrealistic can play a huge part in the failure of a marriage. That is because you are marrying a human, and humans have a way of disappointing us or just changing.

Expectations in most marriages in the nineties reflect the changes in gender roles that have taken place over the last four or five decades. If you question that, go ahead and read the following passage, which appeared in a popular magazine in the fifties:

> The happy wife adapts her mood to her husband's, conceals her disappointments, and puts the big chair by the fire where he wants it even though it spoils the effect she planned. Adaptability means more than weakly giving in. Rather, it means the ability to understand his needs, to see his point of view, and to identify with him so fully that his wishes are usually hers.[1]

Before you laugh off the previous passage, let me point out that these words were published in the January 1955 issue of the *Ladies Home Journal*. Do you think you can find a passage like that in this decade? While we're dusting off old periodicals, brace yourself for the following questionnaire that appeared in the *Journal* in 1952:

> Every good wife wants to live up to her husband's expectations, but some wives feel that their husbands make unreasonable demands. The questions below concern the things that the average husband expects of his wife.
>
> Can he count on you to:
>
> 1. Prepare his breakfast in the morning?
> 2. Serve well-balanced, tasty meals?
> 3. Maintain a tidy, comfortable home?
> 4. Be a wise and thrifty shopper?
> 5. Keep his clothes mended and presentable?
> 6. Be neat and attractive in appearance?
> 7. Fit your schedule to his job demands?
> 8. Help entertain his friends and associates?
> 9. Show respect to his relatives?
> 10. Recognize and adjust to his moods?
> 11. Acknowledge and praise his achievements?
> 12. Talk major problems over with him?
> 13. Be sincerely affectionate and loving?

The magazine went on to offer this analysis: "Most wives answer 12 or all 13 questions positively, and agree that their husbands are justified in their expectations. But unhappy wives rarely score above 10. If your score is less than 11 or 12 affirmative answers, both you and he are missing something in your marriage. Analyze your omissions to see where you can improve."[2]

A TRANSITIONAL GENERATION

What relevance do ragged issues of the *Ladies Home Journal* have today? More than you might imagine! The fifties may be forty years behind us, but measurable traces of that decade continue to simmer between the sexes today.

For all of our heightened social savvy and our political correctness, why do we married people still haggle over who's going to vacuum the carpet or put out the trash? Why do men expect their wives to have careers, and then feel resentful when they can't get everything done around the house? And why do some women expect it all, including a beautiful home, successful spouse, perfect kids, delightful dogs, and a seat on the New York Stock Exchange?

We're all part of a generation touched by the last of (I'm sad to say) a couple of dying breeds: stay-at-home moms and well-defined roles. Some of us grew up in a generation when it was more honorable for women to raise children than conquer careers, a generation where dad moonlighted if necessary so that mom could "train up the kids in the way they should go."

In today's society, image and material possessions have become our priorities. Stay-at-home moms are considered second-class citizens. The American dream of owning a home is out of reach for most single-income families. It takes dual careers and longer hours just to afford a modest home, two driveable cars, and a dishwasher. Consequently, couples see less of each other, kids see less of their parents, and everybody sees more of McDonald's. Some dream!

These are challenging, stressful, and downright confusing times for married couples. But some people compound matters by bringing unrealistic expectations into their relationships, expectations modeled by another generation when those expectations were attainable.

Some husbands, for example, enthusiastically endorse the concept of equality between the sexes (especially on payday), as long as it doesn't interfere with "traditional" wifely duties, such as getting up with sick kids, cleaning the house, paper-training the new puppy, doing the shopping and cooking. They're shocked when she finally says: "Wait a minute! Why am I buried in laundry, shopping lists, kids, dogs, and dust... while you're out golfing every Saturday morning? I work forty hours a week, too."

But men aren't the only ones attempting to reclaim a past modeled for them during childhood. For instance, some women who started careers before starting families suddenly find themselves *torn between their longing to be at home with their children and their desire to maintain a dual-income lifestyle.* They feel cheated out of the opportunity to be full-time nurturers, the way they were nurtured as children. Unfortunately, unless the Hope Diamond magically turns up in their kid's rock collection, most families have priced themselves right out of this experience.

Other women enter a marriage hoping to skip career and go straight to motherhood. The fantasy reads: "I'll be a mom, and my husband will be very successful. He'll come home every evening with a bouquet of flowers or a box of chocolates."

WHAT'S REASONABLE?

How were you touched by your parents' generation? Did you enter your marriage with expectations right out of a "Father Knows Best" rerun? To a certain extent, I did.

Looking back, I had some unreasonable expectations when I got married. For example, I imagined my wife would love to cook. (She doesn't!) I also thought the biggest advantage of married life would be sexual intimacy upon request. (Any married person knows better than that!)

My unrealistic expectations weren't limited to my marriage, but also applied to parenthood. I thought my children would rush to greet me each evening and ask that I read to them from the Bible before dinner. Instead, I'm doing well if they look up from playing Barbie long enough to say "Hi, Dad!"

In 1980, my new role as the "man of the house" seemed straightforward enough: establish a career, mow the yard, build fences, replace shingles, install sprinklers, and dig holes. Anything requiring gasoline, socket wrenches, drill bits, and extension cords would be my department. Everything else was my wife's job.

It finally sank in, though, that my wife couldn't run a household, care for a newborn baby, prepare dinner, and work part-time as a registered nurse without some "inside" assistance. That meant I had to bend my image of our roles. It also meant occasionally doing the laundry, running the vacuum cleaner, mopping, and changing diapers.

It took time, but I discovered that switching on a vacuum cleaner didn't mean switching off my masculinity. As for my wife, she often ventures into the back yard to pull weeds, rescue wilting shrubs, and mow the lawn. She's even used the chain saw once!

Obviously some of the gender roles I grew up believing in went out the window in real life. That can mean a major adjustment for some men, and it did for me.

My answer to this situation, as with other troublesome areas in marriage, is always to: (a) acknowledge the difference between your expectations and the reality, (b) request change in honest and mature dialogue, and (c) let go of what you find you can't change.

In other words, you and your spouse can adjust your expectations if you are ready to communicate what those expectations are. Problems compound, however, when you engage in tactics such as resentment, manipulation, and withholding when things don't go as you think they should.

MISSING THE FOREST FOR THE TREES

Before spending time and energy on a specific expectation, take the time to ask yourself the following questions:

1. *How important is this expectation in my life?*

2. *Is my expectation truly attainable? Truly realistic?*

3. *How disappointed will I feel if the expectation fails to materialize?*

4. *Is my expectation something I could live just as easily without?*

5. *Would it be easier to manage my need, rather than attempting to force an expectation out of an unwilling spouse?*

I first became aware of the expectations of others early in my childhood. My dad had a thing about leaving the lights on in an empty room. Since my dad was a super-stickler about this detail, flipping light switches off became second nature to me. Otherwise, I'd be stuck listening to one of his lectures about people in China without electricity.

Naturally, I entered into marriage with an expectation that my wife would also be light-switch sensitive. What I failed to realize is that she was from a family of twelve, and there was no such thing as a room that wasn't in use. Consequently, a dark room meant only that the light bulb had to be changed.

Initially, I launched into my father's sermon about saving electricity, but that didn't make much difference to my family. As my frustrations grew, sermons became heated discussions. Finally, it occurred to me how crazy this had gotten. I've got a great wife and two wonderful children, and I'm letting a few pennies a day get in the way of my feelings for them.

I realized that I couldn't have a great marriage or set a positive example for our children if I was hung up on trivial things such as saving a few cents on the next electric bill. Sure, I could have drawn a line in the sand. But was it worth the hassle? I don't think so!

How do you determine what issues are worth confronting? Start by asking yourself this simple question: How important is this issue in the context of God's Word?

Here's another question you can ask yourself: If my spouse were to pass away today, would I want our last conversation to be a fight over nothing? I'm not saying to try at all costs to avoid all arguments, disagreements, and heated discussions. Conflicts are unavoidable, even in the best of marriages. But our goal should be to rein in our emotions long enough to weigh the consequences of our words and actions. As my dad used to say as he was patrolling the house for burning lights, "Think before you speak."

After you've examined your feelings, put a temporary lid on your emotions. If you still feel like climbing into the ring with your spouse, then wait for the bell and may the best spouse win. Only remember, what's the point of winning at all costs if it costs you happiness in your marriage?

PLAN FOR HAPPINESS

Why do you think Christ chose to come to earth and walk among us in the first place? To give us high-fives for the terrific job we were doing on earth? Or, as the old adage goes, had we become "our own worst enemies"?

God's example of acceptance and mercy, through love and grace, should be a model for our marriages as well. No question, he has high expectations for us. But he also knows that we're going to stumble along the way. God expects only our love and willingness to follow his Word. Those two things ensure that we're never out of relationship with the Lord.

With that in mind, why do we measure our mates against standards more rigid than those established by God? It hardly seems fair, does it? Maybe it's time to give your spouse the same margin for error that God has given you. Your unrealistic expectations may be a large part of the reason you feel so alone and unhappy in your marriage.

Here are some other examples of how unrealistic expectations might appear in your marriage:

1. **Your expectation:** He'd love to sit and talk with you for hours on end like he did when you were dating.
   Your perception of reality: He would rather watch football or read the sports section than talk to you.
   Reality: While he enjoys talking with you, it's sometimes difficult to find common ground because your interests and schedules are so different.

2. **Your expectation:** You'd go places, take trips, and share quality time.

   Your perception of reality: On weekends, his favorite pastime is sitting in front of the TV or golfing with his buddies.

   Reality: He doesn't think to plan outings, and you gave up when your resentment increased.

3. **Your expectation:** You wanted to marry someone who would be a strong spiritual leader.

   Your perception of reality: Attending church is slightly lower on his priorities than football games.

   Reality: While he is lukewarm on religion, he does lead prayer before meals, and most of the time he takes the family to church without too much coercion.

4. **Your expectation:** She'd lovingly prepare your favorite meals each night of the week.

   Your perception of reality: She isn't interested at all in cooking, and would rather do anything but cook for you.

   Reality: She does cook a couple nights each week when time allows. Like you, she also has a very busy schedule.

5. **Your expectation:** Sexual intimacy would always be instantly available like it was early in the marriage.

   Your perception of reality: Sexual intimacy is usually precipitated by roses, a bottle of champagne, and thirty minutes of begging.

   Reality: It's not really that bad. You just have to adjust more to her timing.

6. **Your expectation:** She'd work part-time and be a wizard at balancing the checkbook and saving money.

   Your perception of reality: Her idea of fiscal responsibility is to buy only two gallons of mayonnaise at the grocery club warehouse.

   Reality: She does bring in some extra money, and if you really knew how much it costs to run a household, you'd probably faint.

As you can see, reality pales in the presence of our lofty expectations. If you've wagered your happiness against unrealistic expectations, you're in for a bumpy ride.

Here are a few common examples of reality versus expectation. Look the list over for similarities in your own marriage.

Your Reality	Your Expectation
I'm a secretary.	I'd be a nurse.
I'm a grocery store clerk.	I'd be a lawyer.
I'm OK as a mom.	I'd be the best mom in the world.
I'd be a great dad, far better than my dad was.	At times I struggle as a dad.
I have to work just to make ends meet.	To be a full-time mom.
My life is boring.	We'd take trips and constantly do fun things.
I'm not very happy.	I'd always be happy and satisfied with my life.
We struggle financially.	My husband would make adequate income.
My kids don't like church.	My kids would love to go to church.
We live in a small house.	I envisioned a nicer, larger home.
We have almost no savings.	I thought we'd be financially set at this point.
We argue too much.	Arguments would be rare and when they occurred, my husband would apologize and make up.
Sometimes, I don't love her.	Romance would always be alive and well.
She doesn't look like she did when we got married.	She'd always look young and physically attractive.

CONTROLLING EXPECTATIONS

Once you've identified your unrealistic expectations in your marriage, you can take steps to banish them from your marriage. Here are a few suggestions:

1. *The second you feel a bout of bitterness coming on over unmet expectations, pray for your partner and yourself.* Pray to God for the strength to deal with the things within your control, while releasing those issues outside of your control.

2. *Take your thoughts captive.* The apostle Paul exhorts us in 2 Corinthians 10:5 to "take captive every thought to make it obedient to Christ." When we fail to understand and control our own thoughts, we are subject to Satan's influence. Face it, the devil loves nothing more than to see us damaging our marriages by comparing our expectations to reality.

3. *If unrealistic expectations or needless comparisons have caused resentment in your marriage, then make the commitment to stop.* Lasting change requires decisive action!

"IF ONLY" THINKING

When expectations continually exceed realities within a marriage, it's a safe bet that one or both partners are actively engaging in "if only" thinking.

As kids, we played the "if only" game to perfection. If only we had the latest toy. If only our parents were more like our friend's parents. If only we had two scoops of ice cream instead of one. Then we'd be happy.

A new bike or a Barbie playhouse. No question about it, if only you had these things, you'd be happy. But even when you finally got what you wanted, were you satisfied? That shiny new bike was awesome—for about a week. The Barbie playhouse was neat, until your friend got the Barbie Corvette. So it was back to the wishing well and another set of "if only's."

Some of us, however, never outgrew this way of thinking, and it is putting tremendous strain on our marriages.

"If only" thinking is a direct path to disappointment and a sure way of distancing you from your spouse. After a while, the spouse on the receiving end of "if only" thinking grows tired of always falling short in that mate's eyes. When we attempt to compare reality with "if only," we're playing the game of childhood wishing again, only the stakes are much higher than a new bike or a new doll.

A successful marriage is one where you train yourself to overlook your spouse's flaws, peculiarities, and faults. After all, your spouse must also overlook your imperfections.

COMPOSITE COMPARISON SHOPPING

A close relative of "if only" thinking takes the form of what I call "composite comparison shopping."

We live in a media-saturated society that encourages comparison. We're asked to compare toothpastes for whiteness, fabric softeners for softness, and laundry detergents for brighter colors. The underlying message is always the same: compare and consume.

We're told to compare, to crave, and ultimately to decide that what we've got needs replacing or upgrading. It may be a productive way to increase sales, but it's a destructive way to live your life.

Making simple comparisons between people can be damaging enough, but husbands and wives often take it a step further by making composite comparisons, mixing and matching attributes to form a fantasy mate.

Men and women are equally guilty of comparison shopping, though they go about it from slightly different perspectives. To better understand these differences, I conducted an admittedly unscientific survey of listeners to my radio talk show. Here were the results:

Men's Priorities	Women's Priorities
1. Physical attractiveness	1. Earning potential (security)
2. Compatibility	2. Compatibility
3. Intelligence	3. Sense of humor
4. Sense of humor	4. Physical attractiveness
5. Earning potential	5. Intelligence

When it comes to comparative shopping, men seem to focus on physical attributes, while women place more emphasis on issues of security. The warning for both sexes is: Chronically comparing your spouse to another can only harm your marriage.

THE MOSAIC SYNDROME

Have you ever found yourself picking apart your spouse, bit by bit, focusing on every flaw, no matter how minute? If you have, you may be taking part in what I call the Mosaic Syndrome.

I came to use the phrase "Mosaic Syndrome" after I thought about my appreciation for art when I was a kid. As a youngster, I marveled at the intricacy of mosaic artistry. I loved how the artist pieced together thousands of shapes to form a breathtaking design. But if one part was missing, it drove me crazy. The entire work was ruined in my eyes. It didn't matter how immense or awe-inspiring the mosaic was, I was riveted on the missing piece. Where did it go? Did the artist know it was missing? Why hasn't somebody replaced it? Don't they realize the value of the art has been diminished?

As I have matured, I have gained deeper insight into the trouble nitpicking and faultfinding can cause in a marriage.

For instance, he fails to notice that she has re-tiled the kitchen counter, but notices that she has forgotten his dry cleaning. Or he compliments her on her dress, then asks how the diet is going.

She secretly resents how he doesn't bring home flowers the way he did earlier in the marriage. She compliments his yard work, but points out he didn't sweep the steps of the front porch. She might even have a problem with his lack of hair.

For example, Catherine freely admitted to being compulsively mosaic-minded, something that nearly cost her a date at the altar with the love of her life.

She recalls meeting nice guys, but always found something wrong with them, usually insignificant things. "I used to think I just had high standards," she said. "They were high, all right. Impossibly high!"

Catherine came to that conclusion three years ago, when she met Jeff.

The two connected instantly. They shared much in common: education, religious values, humor, career and family goals, a zest for outdoor activities. They also shared the ideal marital status: single with no priors.

"I knew right away he was a terrific guy. He brought flowers, he was funny, a real blast to be with," Catherine said.

About a year later, they became engaged and the date was set. Shortly after, Catherine and I met for lunch.

"So, catch me up, Catherine," I said. "Jan and I got your wedding invitation. You must be excited."

She grew quiet, and then sheepishly smiled. "Well, Greg, there is a piece missing. He's bald! Well, not totally bald. Bald enough, though."

"You're serious, aren't you, Catherine?"

I tried to reassure her with the old adage: "God only made so many perfect heads and the rest he put hair on."

"Thanks, Greg. But it's a real problem. It's a part of me I feel terrible about," she said. "But I don't know what to do about it. If it weren't his receding hairline, I know I would have found something else wrong with him."

We began discussing her mosaic way of thinking. By the time the bill came, she realized that she had been using faultfinding subconsciously as a way to keep people from getting too close.

There were other issues to be resolved, such as her fear of rejection. But eventually, Catherine was able to see past Jeff's baldness and enjoy his many attributes.

From time to time, she gives me a call to chronicle her latest example of mosaic thinking.

"Jeff had just finished cleaning the garage, and he did a great job," she said. "But instead of complimenting him on how neat and organized everything looked, I pointed out a hammer that was out of place. Can you believe it? A crummy hammer!

"The good news is that I caught myself in the act. I quickly apologized, and proceeded to heap loads of accolades on my guy. I can't believe how much more constructive it is to look for positive things than it is to pick, pick, pick. I found out that it's lonely at the top."

As Catherine learned, it's important to spend more time and energy observing the good things about her spouse than she did finding fault. She learned how foolish it is to ignore that 95 percent of her husband that is positive, while focusing only on the 5 percent she'd like to change.

A BAD CASE OF THE GIMMES

Couples feeling alone in their marriages—without taking the time to understand the reasons why—often look for a "quick fix," anything to make them feel better. I can't tell you how many couples I've counseled over the years who suffered from severe cases of "The Gimmes."

If you want a great example of the gimmes, think about the last time you took your child shopping. I'm convinced that 60 percent of all begging, moaning, and pleading from children occurs in supermarkets. It's difficult to traverse the cereal aisle, for example, without at least one confrontation over which cereal to buy.

To get what they want, children often begin with a simple yet effective "Pleeezzze." If that doesn't work, they take a stab at manipulation: "I'm not going to be your friend anymore," or "I don't love you anymore." Others haul out the heavy artillery, which consists of crying, screaming, and the ever-popular holding of breath. My personal favorite is when they grab whatever they want from the shelves and hide it in your cart under the lettuce when you're not looking.

Kids are born with the gimmes. It seems that their mission in life is to actively pursue anything that might make their tiny lives more pleasurable. More candy! More toys! More fun! Gimme, gimme, gimme!

But some adults refuse to let go of the gimmes. They crave instant gratification, a quick fix or escape from their troubles. Alcohol, food, shopping binges, and affairs can all fit into this category.

The gimmes can do great damage to our lives, including our marriages. For example, our desire for more possessions can lead to piles of debt, which can be a strain for any couple. And our desire for instant gratification can lead to dissatisfaction, one of the steps on the road to extramarital affairs.

We've all benefited from this desire for more. In fact, God does desire more, both for us and from us. Without our desire for more, we would never have defeated diseases or reached the moon.

Without our desire for more, we wouldn't care about improving our lives and we wouldn't value accomplishment. As with most blessings, this one is mixed: technological and social advances versus never quite being satisfied with our own lives. To be truly happy, you have to manage your desire for more.

How do we manage our desire for more? That's why God gave us willpower. I might want a new computer, but my mind kicks in and says "Stop, buddy, you can't afford one right now." I love chocolate sundaes, but willpower says, "One a week, guy, unless you want to be as big as a house."

No, my name isn't Dr. Grinch. I'm not saying there is anything wrong with fun. I'm all for goal-setting, too. And striving for more *can* have a powerful and positive impact in our lives.

However, merely attaining more is never the key to a happy marriage.

ONE LAST TRIP TO THE FIFTIES

Since we began this chapter by poking a little fun at the fifties, it's only fair that we finish with another timeless piece of advice from a 1954 edition of the *Ladies Home Journal.*

While hoping for the best, be satisfied with improvement. A happy marriage is your goal; if you are moving toward it steadily, don't be discouraged if the rate is sometimes slow.

Above all, remember that the first requirement for achieving a successful marriage is the continuing determination to try. Without that spirit, few marriages would survive. With it, few would fail.[3]

1. Clifford R. Adams, "Making Marriage Work," *Ladies Home Journal,* January 1955, 22.

2. Adams, "Making Marriage Work," *Ladies Home Journal,* February 1952, 28.

3. Adams, "Making marriage work," *Ladies Home Journal,* January 1954, 22.

CHAPTER SIX

Setting Boundaries

"Honey, I'm carpooling with Steve today," Jim said as his ride pulled into the driveway. "The car is drifting to the right some. Out of alignment, I think. Sorry, I forgot to tell you last night. Could you have the garage check it out? Gotta go. Bye."

Terri managed a polite, "Sure honey, I'll take care of it." But as Jim went out the door, she grumbled, "It's not like I have anything else going today. Doesn't he have two good legs? Isn't that what lunch hours are for?"

A list of responsibilities already filled with kids, banking, baking, church work, and multiple loads of laundry was growing longer by the minute. And once again Terri's husband had rearranged her schedule to meet his own needs, giving little or no thought to her plans for the day.

A familiar feeling flooded over her, a feeling that she was little more than his "fetch-and-carry" slave. Once again, Jim had used his old standby line: "Sorry, I forgot to tell you" as he bolted out the door. And once again, it had worked.

It wasn't that Terri minded running errands for her husband. Indeed, she felt that husbands and wives should help each other out whenever possible. What she resented was his demanding style and his inability to use the most basic of common courtesies, such as "please" and "thank you." His thoughtlessness about her schedule, her life, and her interests all led to the inescapable conclusion that he viewed her as nothing more than a housewife with too much time on her hands. This wasn't a partnership, she concluded, but a dictatorship.

Terri felt defensive about her daily routine. Even though she wasn't drawing a paycheck, her role as a full-time mother and homemaker—along with volunteer church work—was both challenging and important. She felt fortunate to be a stay-at-home mom in the nineties (a fact that Jim reminded her of on a weekly basis), but she also felt distanced and alone from her husband. In short, she was tired of being treated as a "go-fer."

The one time Terri had tried to express to her husband how his last-minute requests were sometimes difficult to work into her day, she was soundly shut down with a sarcastic "What's wrong, Terri? Afraid you'll miss one of your soaps?"

That comment hurt badly, but she didn't say a word. Instead, she fantasized about Jim standing in the kitchen, disheveled, unshaven, pots boiling over on the stove, house a mess, kids running amuck, washing machine overflowing. Just then she glides though the front door in her business suit, sets her brief-case down and gives Jim a condescending comment along the lines of "Got wrapped up in those daytime soaps again, huh?"

In many cases, a single event will lead a frustrated or angry marriage partner to take action. For Terri, it was the time her college roommate, Stacey, enlisted her help for her upcoming wedding. The two friends had made plans to meet and go over a selection of possible wedding invitations. Everything was set. Stacey had even asked her boss to allow her a little extra time at lunch to finish the project.

That morning, Jim dropped another unexpected errand in Terri's lap that would cut directly into her planned meeting with Stacey. Terri tried to protest and explain her situation, but Jim made his errand sound like an emergency and Terri's plans like lint on his jacket.

The door slammed behind him. Terri was left standing in her front hall, listening to his car drive away. Tears welled up in her eyes, her jaw clenched in anger. She was sure by now he was whistling down the road, sipping his coffee, oblivious to her pain.

Why couldn't he be more of a partner? Why was it Jim's way or no way? Why did she feel so alone, almost irrelevant as a wife? And when was she finally going to start standing up for herself?

Boundary issues are seldom confined to one area of your life. Your inability to say "no" and set healthy boundaries can spread like a cancer to other areas of your personal and family life.

BOUNDARY PROBLEMS IN MARRIAGE

Boundary and marriage problems are joined like links in a chain. I've never encountered a marriage conflict that didn't somehow involve boundary issues. Often, people feel alone in marriage because one or both partners are either boundary breakers or boundary wimps.

Boundary breakers establish aggressive boundaries that infringe on the limits of their spouses. These people believe in exerting control to let everyone know who's in charge. In some cases, boundary breakers are workaholics who refuse to make more time for their spouses. In other cases, such as Terri's, boundary breakers just expect their needs to come first in the marriage.

Boundary wimps, such as Terri, allow their boundaries to be continually trampled. Eventually, even world-class boundary wimps have their limits. Some boundary wimps begin to resent their station in life and attempt to erect a boundary or two. However, these flimsy limits are usually perceived as requests by the boundary breaker, and are quickly squashed. In short, boundary wimps see themselves as weak and powerless, unable to do anything about the behavior of their boundary-busting spouses. This is exactly how Terri felt.

Unfortunately, some people find themselves attracted to boundary breakers. Lacking maturity, they are initially flattered that a stronger (but not necessarily older) person finds them desirable. They also enjoy the feeling of "being taken care of."

It's a good match for a while. In time, however, most people mature and grow to resent being trapped in the "helpless child" role, the one they've been playing since their own childhood. Eventually, they come face-to-face with the real issue at stake: self-respect.

People trapped in this role feel not only powerless but victimized as well. When this continues over a period of time, it turns into a sense of feeling trapped in loneliness and despair.

Self-respect and boundaries are inseparable. In order to set firm boundaries, you need self-respect. In order to gain self-respect, you need boundaries.

Setting boundaries with your spouse is like exercising after a long period of inactivity. The activity may be enjoyable while you're doing it, but the next morning you can barely get out of bed. Many people stop exercising at this point. Like physical exercise, setting boundaries may feel painful at first, but retracting offers only temporary relief from the pain.

CHECKING YOUR FENCES

Are your boundaries or those of your spouse firmly in place? Or are you beginning to see you may be a boundary breaker or a boundary wimp? To get an idea of where you may stand, take a few minutes to answer the following questions:

1. *Do you find that you try to deflect responsibility onto others when things don't go as expected?*

2. *Do you generally put the needs of others ahead of your own?*

3. *Is it difficult for you to be alone for long periods of time?*

4. *Do people keep after you to do something even after you've said no?*

5. *Do you have a problem with putting things off that you should get done right away? (procrastination)*

6. *Have you ever struggled with overeating?*

7. *Have you ever struggled with spending or shopping in excess?*

8. *Is it hard for you to take on more responsibilities?*

9. *Do you feel as though you owe it to the people you know to be cheerful and helpful and to take care of their needs?*

10. *Do you feel as though people often take advantage of you?*

11. *Are you more impulsive than you'd like to be?*

12. *Do you tend to isolate?*

13. *Do you feel guilty when you say no?*

14. *After you've said no, are there times you change your mind and say yes?*

15. *Do you ever think to yourself, "If only I could be more like him or her, then I'd be happy"?*

If you answered five or more of these questions "yes," you are in need of some boundary repair work. Read on and see where you can make changes in your life in this area.

RIGHTING THE BOUNDARY SHIP

If your marriage is struggling because of boundary issues, then learning how to set and maintain personal boundaries may be your last chance to right the relationship and set it sailing on course.

The thing you need to be most careful of avoiding is giving in to the fear of angering the boundary breaker. Remember, boundary breakers don't respect the territorial rights of others. He or she is going to be upset if you stand up for yourself. But the only way to get a boundary breaker to respect your boundaries is to *earn* that respect. This is best done by requesting respect and later commanding it through consistency in your actions.

In order to learn to set your boundaries, you need to learn the points I've laid out in this chapter.

You've a right to set your boundaries. If you allow your boundaries to be molded and manipulated by others, you lose any sense of self. You become a slave to the needs, wishes, desires, and control of others. Only you can take full ownership of your personal boundary system. Your boundaries encompass who you are as a person in the following ways:

1. *Your boundaries define how you choose to feel as opposed to how others want you to feel.* People with wimpy boundaries often assume the feelings of those around them, even if they totally disagree.

2. *Your boundaries define how you choose to behave versus how <u>others</u> want you to behave.* People with weak boundaries spend an unhealthy amount of time trying to "fit in" or behave the way others would like them to behave.

3. *Boundaries define your personal choices.* Freedom of choice, or free will, is more than a constitutional right; it's a God-given right. Unfortunately, many people usurp God's authority through control and manipulation of others. Your behavior should reflect your own free will while respecting the personal choices of others.

4. *Your values or belief systems are also housed within your personal boundaries.* They are the basis of what's important to you. Regaining your belief system is merely taking ownership of what's already yours, including religious, political, parenting, and social beliefs.

5. *Defining your limits means saying NO to abusers or those people who would take advantage of you.* In other words, it means not enabling others to act irresponsibly or selfishly at your expense.

6. *You're ultimately responsible for meeting your needs.* Don't wager happiness on another's ability to make your life fulfilling. Your most basic needs—to feel loved, bonded, and attached to God and others—are your responsibility.

Expect resistance. When you begin saying "no" for the first time, expect to feel tremendous pangs of guilt. And rest assured, your boundary-breaking mate will also try to play the guilt card.

Guilt can make you believe that everything's your fault, that you're a bad person for looking out for yourself. Before setting protective boundaries, it's important to rid yourself of this way of thinking. After all, this may be the first time you've ever stood up for yourself.

Most wimpy boundary makers fight an uphill battle against years of passive behavior. They must overcome a childhood, adolescence, and adulthood where it wasn't OK to say no.

Be forewarned, your boundary-breaking spouse won't take your first boundaries seriously. He or she will assume you're kidding, even when told otherwise. Your spouse may then counter by switching to the manipulation mode, including a full range of emotions from anger (even rage) to sweetness. He or she might try to convince others that you've been acting strange lately. And look out for the favorite of boundary breakers: the silent treatment.

Real boundaries carry consequences if broken. When a person sets a boundary, he or she also needs to establish consequences for when that boundary is broken by someone.

A well-known biblical boundary with severe consequences is told in the story of Sodom and Gomorrah.

Remember when the angels warned Lot and his family, as they fled Sodom in the face of God's wrath, "Don't look back, and don't stop anywhere in the plain! Flee to the mountains or you will be swept away!" (Gn 19:15, Living Bible).

Unfortunately, Lot's wife broke God's boundary and glanced back at the burning city. "But Lot's wife looked back and she became a pillar of salt" (Gn 19:26).

God's boundaries and limits for our lives were never more apparent than when he said, "Thou shalt not..." How much respect would you have for the Ten Commandments had they been called the "Ten Suggestions" or "Ten Possibilities"? The movie would have starred Don Knotts, not Charlton Heston. The Ten Commandments aren't suggestions or lofty concepts open for debate; they are God's absolute boundaries for our lives.

As you think about the boundaries you need to establish with your spouse, be sure you identify ahead of time what you will do if the boundary is broken. Here's a story about how a wife set boundaries *and* consequences:

Dave and Barbara had signed up for the Wednesday night Bible study class at their church. Since the class started at 7:00 P.M., they had to leave the house by 6:30 to arrive on time. Dave, however, would invariably get "hung up" at the office for one reason or another. As a result, they'd wind up ten to fifteen minutes late for every meeting.

Barbara tried to express her feelings of embarrassment for being late, but Dave paid little attention. Finally, she warned that if he made them late one more time, she was going to Bible study alone. He was welcome to join her when he could, but she was going to be on time.

As usual, her boundary-breaking husband brushed off the warning as another bluff. But when Dave waltzed through the door at 6:50 the following Wednesday, his wife was gone. She had made good on her announced consequences. Dave was never late again.

Boundaries provide protection. Personal boundaries encompass everything we are and would like to become. Our likes and dislikes, our dreams, our prejudices and tolerances, our joys and sorrows, our passions and our ambivalences. Above all, our boundaries tell the world who we are.

As a therapist, my personal boundaries help me keep my patients' problems separate from my own life. Otherwise, their problems are my problems, and nothing would be accomplished.

As you practice setting boundaries in your life, you need to distinguish between what's your responsibility and what falls outside of your jurisdiction.

Don't lose sight of one basic tenet of boundary setting: Boundaries are intended to be defensive and not offensive. When you set boundaries, concentrate on setting them in areas where you are being taken advantage of.

Setting boundaries against inappropriate behavior is never easy. Creating a plan is your best defense against the resistance you'll encounter.

Boundaries are biblical. Some Christians believe that saying no is selfish and un-Christian, and consequently they have difficulty saying no to others, even when it means ignoring a boundary. They mistakenly interpret various scriptural passages as instructing them to put their own needs and feelings aside for another, such as a spouse. For example, they might refer you to Galatians 6:2: "Carry each other's burdens, and in this way you will fulfill the law of Christ." The key word here is *burden,* meaning a crisis. While we are absolutely called to carry each other in times of crisis, it was never meant as a catch-all, covering another person's anger, anxiety, failures, setbacks, or abusive behavior. A few lines later in Galatians 6:5, Paul writes: "For each one should carry his own load."

Some boundaries need to be rigid, but some should remain flexible. God clearly demonstrates that boundaries should be flexible, depending on the situation. In Acts 15:36, Paul rejects Barnabas' request to include John Mark in their travels. Later, in 2 Timothy 4:11, Paul tells Timothy to go find John Mark and bring him back to help with a mission.

When attempting to rebuild a marriage, it's important to communicate scriptural boundaries. Let your yes mean yes and your no mean no, but not necessarily forever. As people change, and become less threatening, your boundaries can be adjusted accordingly.

DETERMINING NEEDS

Only you can determine what your needs are when it comes to setting limits and boundaries. Certainly, there are basic boundaries, such as not tolerating physical abuse.

But you should closely examine your marriage as you search through your list of needs and expectations in order to identify the areas that make you feel the most alone. These are the key areas where boundaries should be established. Your next step is to establish boundaries in those areas.

WHAT IF I MARRIED A BOUNDARY BREAKER?

I've been discussing how to begin a life with personal boundaries. But what if you are already married to a boundary breaker? How do you survive while in the process of learning to set boundaries?

Finding support. Whenever you begin setting boundaries, especially if it's for the first time in your life (or marriage), be sure there is a support system in place. Find a close friend, a pastor or a therapist to talk to. Find somebody to provide positive feedback and motivation to continue your hard work.

Scripture tells us it's wise to have a multitude of counselors. It may be beneficial to have several sessions with a Christian counselor or a pastor prior to embarking on your boundary voyage. **Note:** If, for whatever reason, you have to see a secular counselor, be aware that his or her values may differ from yours. This person may see your marriage situation as hopeless and counsel you to separate.

Safe people are those with sound ethics and value systems, such as trusted friends, relatives, or pastors. Choose people who demonstrate good boundaries, which are not to be confused, mean-spirited, or offensive boundaries.

You might also contact larger churches in your area. Ask

them if they conduct support groups relating to boundary skills. For example, some may have codependency groups that will be useful. If you can't find a group like that, call around to the local hospitals that offer drug and alcohol treatment programs. They are usually helpful in pointing you in the direction of groups and classes in your area.

Patience and confidence. When embarking on a boundary-setting mission, resist the temptation to race ahead. For instance, if you think your wife has an alcohol problem, don't make your first boundary something like, "If you don't stop drinking, I'm leaving." Begin by starting communication about the particular issue. Never set a boundary until the issues have been openly discussed.

For instance, you could introduce the topic with a question: "Should I be concerned with your drinking?" or "I'm worried about how much you are drinking. I'd like to talk about it with you after you've had a chance to think." In psychological terms, this is called "preparing the patient."

When it does come time to set your first boundary, do so with confidence. I've observed that most people have greater success when they follow these steps:

1. *Before moving forward with your boundary, consider these mandatory prerequisites:*
   - The boundary must be set out of love.
   - The boundary must be defensive and not offensive.
   - The boundary is placed to improve the other person, yourself, and the relationship.
   - Talk your potential boundary over with someone you trust. Determine if your boundary is reasonable and fair. Are you justified in setting the boundary, or are you overstepping your boundaries in the process?

2. *Examine your motives and goals in setting the boundary.* If they are to rebuild the relationship, decide if the boundary is right to accomplish the goal.

3. *Pick your place as carefully as you choose the time* to discuss personal boundaries with your spouse. Boundary setting should never be done publicly.

4. *Anticipate your mate's reaction* to any new boundary. Have contingency plans in place. Don't be closed to the possibility of negotiating an area where he or she isn't yet ready to accept your boundary.

5. *Practice your boundary-setting with someone safe.* Role-play to get feedback on how you are coming across. Are you too pushy, too angry, or too meek?

6. *When it's time to communicate your boundary, do it clearly and concisely.* State your case in an orderly way, omitting superficial information. Don't stockpile old weapons to launch at your mate. Just state your case with "I" statements. Make it very clear why you are requesting his or her compliance and carefully consider the response.

7. *Ask for compliance.* In sales, it's called "asking for the sale." This should be done before any consequence is discussed.

8. *Whenever you've set a boundary, give the other person a chance to process the information.* Generally, twenty-four hours is appropriate. You might even suggest he or she "sleep on it" before further discussions are held.

9. *If your spouse is unwilling to comply with your boundary, he or she has left you little choice but to set a consequence.* Before you set a consequence, make sure that:

- The consequence fits the problem.
- You are prepared to be firm with your consequence.
- You calmly define the consequence for him or her.
- You tell him or her again why the boundary is important to you.
- You follow through with the consequence if you are forced to.

TERRI ESTABLISHES A PERSONAL BOUNDARY

We opened this chapter with the story of Terri. Let's finish with the rest of her story.

Over time she came to the place where she was willing to establish some personal boundaries. She finally made an "official" dinner date with Jim. She didn't divulge the subject matter in advance, only that it was a very serious topic and that she wanted no interruptions. That was a personal boundary in itself.

Over dinner, Terri's tone was soft-spoken and complimentary. "You know, honey, you're good at your job," she said. "You know how to give orders, delegate work, stay organized, and work as a team.

"I've heard more than once," she continued, "that you're a good listener, that you treat everybody with respect. I'm not asking that you do something you're incapable of doing, only that you do them within our marriage as well."

Jim nodded and listened attentively as Terri got to the heart of the issue.

She produced her daily planner. "I know this won't be necessary in the future, but I'd like you to take a look at what my schedule looks like."

Her husband flipped through the pages. Almost every block of time was filled. She gently explained that she felt hurt and belittled when he ordered her around with little regard or respect for her schedule.

"And those soap opera cracks? Those are really low blows."

Taking her hand across the table, Jim recounted the time she had been sick in bed for two days with the flu.

"Remember, I had to make the dinner, fix the lunches, and take the kids to school," he said. "Remember when I ran the dishwasher with regular dish soap? There was a river of suds from the kitchen to the family room. I was never so glad as when you got back on your feet. Thank you for reminding me."

He apologized for ordering instead of asking, and for taking her everyday activities for granted. He promised to stop dropping last minute bombs, especially those he knew about and could handle himself.

They ended their dinner with a toast to their mutually improved respect and love for each other. Terri was ready to stand up for herself and make her boundaries stick. And, just as importantly, Jim was willing to respect them. Isn't that what marriage is all about?

CHAPTER SEVEN

Communication Breakdowns

If there is one thing couples with marital difficulties have in common, it is the inability to communicate. For some reason, they just can't talk to one another like they used to. Catch-all phrases such as "We just don't talk anymore" seem ridiculously trite and vague, but the loss of communication is no doubt at the core of most divorces.

There are all kinds of communication problems, many of them related, but all with their own unique characteristics. Learning to accurately identify and understand these communication snafus can jump-start the healing process in your marriage.

No question, communication is the cornerstone to any successful marriage. Our needs, desires, hopes, and dreams hinge on an open exchange of feelings. Without that exchange, feelings go unexpressed and expectations unfulfilled. Personal boundaries crumble and intimacy suffers. Without that exchange, the smallest emotional speed bump becomes a major obstacle to a happy marriage.

For an illustration of what can happen when communication breaks down, read on:

NOTHING TO CROAK AT

"A pond? In our back yard?" Ann couldn't believe what she was hearing. She was certain that she and her husband had agreed that they would put a small rose garden in the yard to finish off the landscape.

But Tim, her husband, was undaunted. "Won't it be great!" he said, his eyes widening as he pointed to a weedy plot located directly outside their bedroom window. "It's absolutely the perfect place for a pond! Sort of romantic, too—the sound of water and everything."

"Nice try," Ann muttered under her breath. She imagined the worst: a mosquito-infested slime pit, crawling with all sorts of unidentifiable life forms. Despite her misgivings, she agreed to the new addition.

Tim eagerly threw himself into the project, working tirelessly every evening—often well after dark—shoveling a small mountain of dirt from an elongated five-foot hole.

And it wasn't long before the pear-shaped depression was transformed into a sparkling pool, ringed by flagstone and landscaped with rocks, ferns, and flowers. Japanese koi soon circled beneath the water lilies that skimmed the surface.

Despite her initial protests, Ann had to admit that the pond had become a beautiful centerpiece of the back yard. Kids came from all over the block to feed the fish. Even her parents, who basically hated anything having to do with pets, raved about the pond.

Everything was going beautifully until Tim scooped four tiny tadpoles from the nearby park and released them into his waterscape. Even that was no problem—until the tadpoles did what tadpoles naturally do: develop into full-fledged frogs.

Soon, the frogs started showing their appreciation for life in general by croaking all night, every night. These were not pleasant-sounding background croaks, but belching blasts that kept Ann awake night after night. Tim, a heavy sleeper, remained unconscious through these midnight serenades.

After several sleepless nights, Ann realized that this couldn't go on. Somehow, she had to get some sleep, and that wasn't going to happen with those frogs living right outside the bedroom window. She attempted to rationally discuss the problem with Tim during breakfast one morning, but he kept his face buried in the sports section, shrugging her off with a barely audible grunt.

"Overreacting again," he thought, without looking up from his paper. "If the frogs are making such a racket, how come I never hear them? She must be getting close to her period."

Ann repeatedly attempted to communicate her feelings to her husband, but with no success. It was only a matter of time before a major communication land mine would detonate. For Ann, that explosion came one evening when Tim remarked over dinner that she was "looking a little haggard lately."

Without saying a word, Ann left the table and prepared the spare bedroom for a new guest—herself! While switching bedrooms solved one problem—a lack of sleep—it created another one by driving a wedge of tension and isolation between Ann and her husband.

Every evening, Ann would dutifully give her husband a good night kiss, then retire to the guest room. And every evening, much to her disappointment, Tim would let her go. "If only he would ask me to come back to bed with him," she thought. "Then we could work this out."

But Ann and Tim had become involved in an emotional standoff, with each person stubbornly waiting for the other to make the first move toward a truce. But there was truly no compromise in sight.

"How easily he disregards my feelings. What if something really major happened? How would he react then?" she wondered.

From Ann's perspective, it was obvious that Tim cared more about his pond than he did for their marriage. But who was she kidding? She realized that she had begun feeling neglected and alone in the marriage even before the pond incident. Tim had stopped doing the little things that communicated his love for her. She thought longingly back to a time when Tim did things such as open her car door, pull out her chair when they were seated at a restaurant, offer her a soda when he got one for himself, wait until she was finished with her meal before jumping from the dinner table and plopping down on the couch to watch the ball game.

The way Ann saw it, the pond controversy was just another impeaching piece of evidence that Tim really wasn't interested in her feelings or needs. After all, it didn't seem to bother him at all that she had moved out of their bedroom!

"If that's the way he wants it, fine!" she said to herself. "I have to make a stand, and I'm making it! But I'm also sleeping alone, feeling alone and unloved. Great point, huh? You showed him!"

AN OLIVE BRANCH

Sooner or later, something had to give in this standoff between Tim and Ann. Either there was going to be an escalation of the hostilities or someone would swallow his or her pride and make an effort to get the problem resolved.

On the fourth night of their separation, just as Ann was getting ready for bed, Tim asked her if she would like to discuss their problems. They talked about how Ann felt when Tim shut her out when she tried to explain that the frogs were keeping her awake. They also talked about how she felt when he let her go sleep in the guest bedroom.

Together, they worked out a plan of action to resolve their problems, including moving the pond away from their bedroom.

But there was more to the problem than the pond. For starters, Ann explained to her husband that she didn't appreciate how he wrote off her feelings about the noisy frogs as nothing more than a monthly hormonal imbalance. She pointed out that this was not the first time he had done that. She also told him that it belittled her feelings, causing her to become even more angry with him. Tim agreed and apologized for the insensitive remark he had made.

With that little hurdle behind them, Ann continued to openly and calmly discuss her feelings with her husband, feelings she had kept buried for much too long.

Over the next few weeks, Tim and Ann worked together digging a new pond, adding new plants, and even installing decorative lights at Ann's suggestion. As for the pond's prior location, that became the small rose garden that Ann had always wanted. Meanwhile, the frogs continued to croak—from a muffled distance.

AN EPILOGUE

Tim and Ann finally worked out their differences when Tim took the initiative to call a cease-fire and approach his wife, asking for the lines of communication to open. His wife—unwilling or unable to initiate this process herself—was nonetheless ready and willing to respond to him. While it is always a positive thing when two people work out their differences, problems such as those endured by Tim and Ann can be avoided if communication is kept open.

But should—or can—a marriage be completely free of conflicts in communication? Of course not. That would mean that both parties had disengaged both emotionally and verbally.

The key to effectively resolving our conflicts is direct communication, such as Ann and Tim finally displayed. Let's begin by discussing what *doesn't* work when it comes to communication in a marriage where one or both partners are feeling alone.

COMMUNICATION CONFLICTS AT THEIR UGLIEST

Can you imagine what it would be like if all husbands and wives were willing and able to openly and honestly communicate their feelings and hurts to one another, then work their problems out the same way? If that were the case, there would be no need for this or any other marriage repair book.

Unfortunately, there will always be communication conflicts in marriages. That is because many of us don't know how to effectively and honestly communicate as we should.

I have listed some of the uglier forms of communication and attempted to illustrate by example what they can look like. See if you recognize any of these ugly forms of communication in your marriage relationship:

Manipulation. Frank was an unparalleled procrastinator. Whenever his wife, Mary, brought up a household chore, Frank had an excuse ready. It seemed to Mary as though there was always something Frank had to do before mowing the lawn, cleaning the garage, or finishing the door he started painting in 1992.

Naturally, Mary often became frustrated with her husband. But instead of openly discussing her feelings of resentment and disappointment, Mary manipulated. When Frank didn't finish painting the door, she bought paint supplies and stacked them atop the TV. When he ignored this not-so-subtle hint, she got angry and start painting the door herself.

When nothing happened when she tried to get Frank to clean the garage, she asked her father to help her move some heavy items. You can imagine her husband's feelings when his father-in-law came to his home to help his wife with one of his chores!

When all of her manipulations failed, Mary would break out the heavy artillery: the silent treatment. She'd ignore Frank, sometimes for days, until he finally discovered why every shirt he owned had come back from the dry cleaners with extra starch.

Clearly, manipulation circumvents communication. It keeps us from communicating our needs in a direct and honest fashion. Certainly, Frank was not an innocent victim in this scenario.

But the real issue—procrastination—was obscured by the way Mary punished her husband through manipulation.

Negativity. We've all heard the expression, "It's not what is said but how it's said that counts." How true, especially in troubled marriages where common courtesies such as "please" and "thank you" have been replaced with rudeness and negativity.

I remember one couple who entered marriage counseling with issues concerning sexual intimacy. Specifically, the husband was interested in intimacy on a daily basis, while the wife seemed completely uninterested in sex.

Instead of approaching the problem with warmth and sensitivity, he resorted to sarcasm. His favorite line as they were getting ready for bed was, "I suppose you've got a headache again, don't you?"

A mature, positive approach would have been, "I'd really like for us to make love more often. Can we discuss it, honey?" But people with difficulties expressing themselves honestly often use negativity instead. It's less risky than openly airing their feelings and facing possible rejection.

Nagging. Whether it's in parenthood or marriage, nagging is an ugly form of communication that seldom achieves the desired effect. People usually nag if they feel they're not being taken seriously enough. Of course, the more they nag the more they're ignored, which perpetuates the cycle.

Webster's says nagging is "to annoy by continual scolding, faultfinding, complaining, urging, etc." Contrary to the stereotype, men and women can be equally proficient practitioners of the art of nagging. From what I've observed, men nag their wives for things they do, such as excessive shopping. On the other hand, women nag their husbands for things they don't do, such as failing to finish a household project.

Is there any hope for someone who is addicted to nagging? My advice is to stop, think, and respond to a situation before you press the nagging button. I also suggest asking yourself if *you* enjoy being nagged. Does it work when someone treats you that way, or does it just make you angry and defiant?

Reacting versus responding. Typically, we stumble over communication land mines when we fail to listen and fully understand what our spouse is really saying. Rather than waiting for the thought process to kick in, we react emotionally by lashing out. The Bible describes this situation like this: "A fool gives full vent to his anger, but a wise man keeps himself under control"(Prv 29:11).

Some people react by slamming their spouse with a barrage of personal insults and "low blows." Others might attempt to shout their spouse into submission. In contrast, a passive spouse reacts to the identical situation by withdrawing, sulking, becoming defensive, or isolating. Regardless of the personality type, reacting can leave your marriage emotionally bankrupt.

As you strive to restore communications in your marriage, be alert for the warning signs that you are reacting, rather than responding. Ask yourself the following questions:

- *Does your face feel flushed?*
- *Have your listening skills shut down?*
- *Do you feel yourself becoming defensive?*
- *Are you already thinking of retaliating?*
- *Is your anger building?*

If you answer "yes" to any of these questions, then you are reacting to a situation rather than responding.

Since this may have been a lifelong habit, it may take time for you to learn to stop reacting and start responding. The best approach is to discuss this ugly form of communication with your spouse and lead by example. Force yourself to stop or call a time out. Always listen carefully and ask clarifying questions.

After that, take a few deep breaths and assess the risk. Ask yourself, do you want to risk a setback at this time? Try your best to deal with the situation using love and logic instead of emotions and reactions.

Proverbs 15:1 tells us: "A gentle answer turns away wrath, but a harsh word stirs up anger."

Dredging up the past. I once counseled a couple who had made digging up past mistakes and hurts an art form. Each time they argued, the wife would remind her husband of the affair he had confessed to several years earlier.

For her, bringing up his past infidelity was more of a defensive measure than an offensive one. She dredged up the past like that to distract her husband from pointing out her faults.

When you must argue with your spouse, play fair by not pulling out old ammunition. Stick to the subject. Don't dredge up the past. Work through past emotional injuries and then be done with them.

Getting personal. Callers to my radio talk show don't always agree with my opinions. That's fine. I think a little debate is a healthy thing. But on occasion, some callers resort to personal attacks to make their point. "You're an idiot, Greg!" or "I can't believe you call yourself a Christian!" are two prime examples.

Personal insults, whether they are "on the air" or in the kitchen, are an ugly form of communication. Name-calling, slurs, derogatory remarks, and sarcasm have no place in healthy, mature relationships of any kind. These comments also communicate to your spouse that you've lost your composure. At that point, you have lost any chance you had to discuss a situation and work it out like an adult.

Needing to be right. As the expression goes, "Nobody likes a know-it-all." Unfortunately, some of us are married to them. Whether it's baseball or bird feeders, they're the last word on any subject.

Evidently, it's a communication contaminant that's been around for a long time. For example, Paul addressed the issue in

1 Corinthians 8:2: "The man who thinks he knows something does not yet know as he ought to know."

Assuming superior knowledge slams the door on meaningful dialogue in a marriage. Have you ever noticed how a child will argue, argue, argue—never conceding a point? Even as that child leaves, he reels off a few parting shots. If you're a know-it-all, it's time to grow up. Every disagreement with your spouse doesn't have to be a battle to the death. Mature adults agree to disagree. Besides, it isn't necessary to always be right. It's sometimes better just to "drop it."

Presumption. I believe that many of us subconsciously miss the days when our only responsibility was to eat and breathe and let mom take care of every other detail. What a life! Never having to communicate a single word and always having your needs met.

But I also believe that some adults don't outgrow this way of thinking. Some of us simply assume that our spouses know what we want or need to be happy. Married people think things like, "I shouldn't have to tell him that I need help around the house," or "Doesn't she know that I like to go to the ball game with my friends once in a while?"

This may come as a shock to some married people, but the answer to those questions is NO! Your spouse can't possibly know what you need or want if you don't tell him or her!

It's perfectly reasonable to have needs and wants, but waiting for your spouse to be a mind reader is obviously unreasonable. If you want or need something, SAY IT!

Baiting. Some spouses are absolute masters at baiting their mates into confrontations. Still others are good at taking that bait.

For instance, a husband walks through the door, looks at a pile of clothes that just came out of the drier and says, "What have you been doing all day?" The bait is presented, and he's just waiting for his wife to walk into an argument. Now it's decision time. She can take the bait and get into a heated argument over how she spends her time, or she can choose to ignore it, which is clearly the tougher of the two decisions. The correct response would be to respond to his comment by saying, "Are you looking for an argument? Why don't we discuss this later if you still want to?"

If your spouse tries to lure you into an argument and you can't resist the bait, don't thrash around too much. Resisting only sets the hook deeper. Tell your spouse that you're willing to talk about the situation, but that you don't want to argue. The hook will drop freely from your mouth, and all of the sport from this little fishing adventure will be gone.

Abusive truths. A man once sought my counsel over whether to tell his wife about his physical attraction for another woman. He asked me if it was a sin not to tell her about his lustful thoughts.

This sounded suspicious to me, so I pressed him to find out what his motives were for making such a disclosure. He thought for a moment, then admitted that he wanted to get his wife to pay more attention to his sexual needs and to take better care of her appearance.

I pointed out to him that while his needs were valid, his methods were ill-advised, manipulative, and insensitive. I then suggested some more positive ways to encourage his wife toward intimacy with him.

What this man wanted to do was use what I call "abusive truths" to get his wife to do what he wanted. Yes, he was physically attracted to another woman, and yes, that was definitely wrong. But his reasons for telling his wife had nothing to do with his desire to be a faithful, loving husband. He wanted to scare his wife into doing what he wanted. I can only imagine the damage that would have come to that marriage had he gone ahead with his plan.

They say that "actions speak louder than words," but words can cripple communication. The apostle Paul cautions us to "take all thoughts captive." That means that you don't always have to act on or say everything you're thinking. I'm not encouraging you to lie, but to consider the ramifications of being "painfully" honest.

Stare-out. Can you remember the last time you said something encouraging or complimentary to your mate for no particular reason?

As children, many of us had those monumental stare-outs with our friends. They seemed to last forever, until somebody finally blinked or broke up laughing. It's similar to that when married couples engage in emotional stare-outs, but the end result is nothing to laugh about.

When neither spouse is willing to issue the first compliment—any kind of compliment—it becomes a communication stare-out of sorts. Who's going to be kind first? Who's going to blink? The difference is, if nobody blinks, you both lose.

MAKING CHANGES

I've outlined some of the most common and troublesome of communication styles that afflict marriages. But there are literally hundreds of spin-offs and combinations of these styles. The point is that you need to identify what style best describes you and your spouse.

Has your communication style served you well in your marriage? If not, then you must make a decision to change it.

Your communication style falls within your boundary system. But what about your spouse's communication style? Can you force him or her to alter it? Of course not. You can, however, gain a better understanding of how your communication style might be damaging your marriage.

You can disarm your mate's hiding styles by becoming a safe person, which means approaching your relationship from a position of grace and forgiveness. The next time you and your spouse disagree, watch for his or her hiding techniques. Make your spouse secure enough to give up the defense. The goal is to draw your spouse out of hiding and into mature and loving communication.

Hopefully, you now have a better idea of some of the ugly communication styles that may be affecting your marriage. Armed with this knowledge, you are now in a better position to improve marital communication.

THE CONFLICT RESOLUTION POP QUIZ

The next time you feel a conflict approaching, stop and ask yourself the following questions:

1. What are my motives in confronting the problem?
- Do I genuinely care about this person?
- Is he or she just getting on my nerves?
- Am I looking for someone to dump on?
- Am I doing this to help the other person grow?
- Am I doing this out of love?
- Am I honestly communicating a need I have?

2. Am I sure God is directing me to confront?
- Am I open to letting the Holy Spirit deal with my spouse without my help, or am I wrestling God for the honor of confronting him or her?
- Am I willing to pray for my spouse and myself before I confront?

3. Is it something I could let go?
- Is he or she just having a bad day or week?
- Am I making too big a deal over this?
- What would happen if I let it go?

4. *Have I examined my life in the area I'm confronting?*
   - Am I being hypocritical?

5. *Have I really tried to understand?*
   - Have I tried to empathize with my spouse's situation prior to confronting him or her?
   - Why is this so important to my spouse?

6. *Do I have the right to confront?*
   - Is the relationship strong enough at this time to talk about this?
   - Should I let this go until the relationship is in a better place?

7. *Do I have my facts straight?*
   - Is it possible that I'm wrong?
   - Could he or she be seeing a side to this that I'm missing?

8. *Is my mouth in drive while my brain is in park?*
   - Have I examined both positions before confronting?
   - Have I sought the counsel of others if I'm confused?
   - Am I reacting instead of responding?

9. *Am I considering the consequences?*
   - What are the best-case and worst-case scenarios of my actions?
   - Could this permanently damage our relationship?
   - If he or she won't listen, what am I willing to do?
   - Am I willing to take the risk?

10. *Is this confrontation unavoidable?*
    - Will the confrontation be in private?
    - Is the timing right?

SOME FINAL DO'S AND DON'TS:

DO'S

Do actively listen! Do be honest! Do apologize when you are wrong! Do agree to disagree when a resolution isn't apparent! Do talk about your feelings by making "I" statements! Do pray for wisdom in your relationship! Do seek counsel if necessary! Do forgive in abundance!

DON'TS

Don't dominate the conversation! Don't stockpile evidence! Don't make it personal! Don't hold grudges!

And don't wait too long before putting some of these concepts into action. You once opened your heart to your mate. It's time to open it again.

CHAPTER EIGHT

Changes That Heal

Several years ago, I attended this incredibly dull business management seminar. It was one of those affairs where you come out of it without really remembering anything you heard.

But one of the speakers at the seminar delivered a line that managed to stick: "People don't plan to fail, they just fail to plan." She explained the value of creating a written business plan before starting any new venture, a plan that outlined expectations and methods for achieving those objectives.

I didn't know it at the time, but that same concept would one day become an integral tool in helping couples achieve their marital objectives. In other words, I have found that there is a much better chance of a marriage being repaired if the unhappy couple has a detailed plan to turn things around.

How about you? Do you have a plan in mind as you begin making positive changes in your marriage? Or are you just "taking it one day at a time" without any tangible goals? While it is true that you need to put your trust in God and allow him to guide you, there is still a need for planning. These plans shouldn't be written in stone, but you need to have some kind of blueprint as you begin making life changes.

Many couples bring only a sketchy idea of what they hope to achieve into their marriage counseling. They express wishes and desires such as, "I just wish our relationship felt like it did when we were first married." That is a valid goal, to be sure, but it is also a vague one. In some ways, goals like that are worse than no goals at all, because they can set people up for failure.

In counseling, I usually suggest that clients start by taking a pen and paper and writing down their marital goals. I believe that getting your thoughts down on paper enables you to better visualize and focus on your goals. It helps you to develop a game plan for accomplishing what you want to accomplish. Also, having something in black and white allows you to monitor your progress. That way you can make mid-course corrections if needed or stay the course if everything is going according to plan.

ASKING FOR GOD'S HELP

Before I outline the plan, let me remind you that God wants your marriage to work! Are you working with him or against him?

Imagine that he is watching you to see how you are responding to his intervention and assistance. What things will he notice that will affirm his efforts to heal your marriage?

Now that you have a picture that God is your partner in repairing your marriage, what are you going to do differently right away? Ask yourself, what two small things can I do differently today that will affirm to God that I appreciate his help?

Going to God in prayer for yourself, your spouse, and your marriage is an integral step in the healing process. Some may think, "I've asked God to repair my marriage before and nothing has happened." I don't doubt you've asked God to change things, but what changes did you envision? Were they about you or your spouse?

This time, be specific. Ask God to give you the strength and courage to change what *you* can change. Ask that he take control over what is outside of your boundaries. And don't forget to pray for patience. Don't expect too much, especially over a short period of time. Striving for perfection will only undo all of your good work. Be reasonable in your expectations of change. Even after positive changes are made, don't assume things will always be a bed of roses. All marriages have their peaks and valleys. There will be setbacks. The window of opportunity will open and close more than once. Keep your eyes open for those positive openings.

WHAT'S BUGGING YOU?

Before you can effectively set goals for changing your marriage, you and your spouse need to take the time to decide exactly what it is you want or need to change.

This is such a basic step that some people overlook it. But it is amazing how not properly defining your marital problems can hinder your working them out.

For example, an acquaintance of mine from church told me that some of the problems in her marriage had to do with "affection." To her, affection meant nonsexual relating, such as holding hands, hugging, and kissing. For her husband, affection meant one thing: more sex.

I explained to her that until she and her husband came to some agreement on the definition of "affection," there was little or no chance that she would be able to communicate to her mate that she wanted more affection. In a case like this, it would be like going to your doctor because you are in pain, then not telling him exactly where it hurt. The doctor could give you something to temporarily ease the pain, but the cause of the pain would remain undiagnosed.

When you are working to repair or improve your marriage, you need to be specific about what you see as the problems and what you see as the solutions. You should also be specific when discussing your goals in achieving those solutions.

AN EXERCISE IN GOAL SETTING

In order to help you plan your marriage restoration more effectively, you'll need to get some input from your spouse. Start by making a date with your spouse for dinner, a cup of coffee, or some other activity that promotes communication. When the timing seems right, initiate the conversation by saying something like:

> You know, I've been thinking about our relationship. I'm feeling distant from you and I want to recapture the closeness we felt when we were first married. I know that I love you, but I really don't know how you feel about our marriage. What do you need from *me* to be happier?

Use your own words, but remember to avoid putting your spouse on the spot or making him or her feel at fault for your marital problems. If the other person feels that you are placing blame on him or her, then you are likely to run into severe resistance.

After opening this subject for discussion, give your spouse a chance to respond. Don't be surprised or hurt if he or she says something like, "I haven't given it much thought." Also, don't be shocked if you receive the most common response: a blank stare followed by "What?" Above all, keep in mind that your spouse is likely to feel discomfort at this line of communication, simply because it probably hasn't been approached in your relationship.

Once the initial shock subsides, ask your spouse to write down two things you could do to make him or her happier. Ask for the first that springs into his or her mind. Let your spouse know that you will accept and respect any answer he or she gives. That way he or she will be less tempted to mentally edit the response.

Remember to resist the urge to defend yourself when your spouse tells you what he or she would like. If you get defensive, you have pushed the process back even more. Always validate the feelings of your partner when that person shares them.

For instance, your husband might say, "I wish you would spend more time fixing yourself up." Instead of viewing this as a criticism of your appearance, look at it as his way of expressing how much he appreciates your appearance when you spend a little more time on yourself. If he says, "I wish you'd initiate sex more often," don't be defensive. Again, rather than hearing this as a criticism, choose to look at it as his enjoyment of being intimate with you.

Your wife might say, "Honey, I wish you would spend more time with me, instead of always turning on the TV." Rather than hearing this as an attempt to make you miss your favorite sporting event, choose to hear that she enjoys your company and would like to talk to you more.

Again, be as specific as possible when you discuss the two items your spouse has presented. Progress will come to a halt if you fail to fully understand the needs in question. For example, let's say that the first item on his or her list concerns your appearance. Ask your spouse what you can do to make yourself more attractive.

After you've discussed the two items your spouse listed in detail and asked clarifying questions, it's time for action. First, ask yourself if the two requests are realistic and attainable. If so, be sure you are willing to leave your comfort zone to meet those needs. Remember, now that you have asked what your spouse's needs are, he or she will be expecting you to make an effort to meet those needs.

PRESENTING YOUR NEEDS

Once you have taken the time to understand your spouse's needs, it is your turn to present two needs of your own. Just like you asked your spouse to do, go with the first two needs that come to mind.

By all means, resist any desire you may have to make instant changes in your mate. At this stage, your goals are simply to get both of you used to talking about your respective needs *and* to get both of you used to hearing each other's needs. You will be surprised how far a little success in meeting these two simple goals will go in helping you to feel less alone in your marriage!

Keep in mind that it is entirely possible that your spouse will continue to ignore your needs, even as you are working overtime to meet his or hers. If that happens, don't give in to the temptation to quit attempting to meet your spouse's needs. Chalk it up as a show of good faith. Be prepared for your spouse to be skeptical at first. After all, the two of you meeting and understanding each other's needs is a new event in this marriage. Give your spouse a chance to become a team player in this positive exercise.

Also, don't be modest as you make an effort to meet your spouse's needs. Let your mate know how hard you're trying. Let him or her see and acknowledge your efforts.

WHAT WILL CHANGE LOOK LIKE?

As you are attempting to meet your spouse's needs, don't expect that he or she will suddenly make meeting your every need his or her top priority.

As this process of marriage restoration begins, success isn't measured by what your spouse does or doesn't do. At first, success can be measured *solely* on how you're responding in the relationship.

You must be willing to give this process some time. In the meantime, you need to continue making positive changes in yourself. I have listed some positive changes that you can look to make.

- You are more in control of your emotions.

- You are responding instead of reacting to your spouse.

- You are more upbeat and positive about your relationship.

- You are resisting being baited into arguments.

- You are giving without an expectation of receiving.

- You are more pleasant to be around.

- You are doing random acts of kindness for your spouse.

- You are trying harder to be intimate with your spouse, not just sexually but spiritually and emotionally as well.

As you read through this list, is there something that seems conspicuous by its absence? That's right. There is *nothing* about your mate's behavior in this list. That is because your first responsibility in this relationship is you! Without taking responsibility for yourself in your marriage, *nothing* is going to improve.

THE RECTANGLE SOLUTION

As you gain insight and create positive change within yourself, you can envision your image of success as you keep moving toward your goal of a better marital relationship!

But what should be your next step if your spouse seems immovable in his or her resistance to change in your marriage?

A man once approached me after church in search of solutions to this very problem. He complained that the biggest problem in his marriage revolved around his wife's excessive arguing and lack of affection. As far as he could see, it seemed that nothing he could do would change the situation.

"It's not like I haven't tried," he explained. "I've tried to stop fighting with her. I asked her to call a cease-fire, but the truce didn't last. Before long we were at each other's throats worse than ever!"

As I would have expected, this couple's arguing put a quick stop to any affection between the two. Nobody wants to be close to a person that they have a hard time living with!

I walked my friend through a program that I call the

Rectangle Solution, a simple technique in marriage counseling that gets a couple back to basics in their approach to their relationship. This technique is especially effective when one spouse resists the other's attempts to improve the marriage.

The Rectangle Solution is a four-part (hence the name) personal exercise in which you can take stock of what is happening in your marriage, thus gaining insight into how to improve the situation. The four parts are as follows:

1. Gaining perspective. This first step in the Rectangle Solution requires that you envision the marriage from a neutral perspective. In other words, you need to look at your problems without placing blame on yourself or your spouse. On a sheet of paper, write down a list of questions you may have concerning your marriage. These questions should be along the following lines:

- *What's really going wrong here?*

- *Are these all my spouse's problems?*

- *When did our problems seem to get worse?*

- *What have I tried in the past to fix the situation?*

2. Clean up your own mess. If your kids are anything like mine, you've experienced denial and finger-pointing at clean-up time. "That's not my mess!" or "I'm not putting it away!" are common protests from children when it comes time to tidy up the house.

But we adults also resist claiming our own messes, especially when it comes to marital issues. When someone points out one of our messes, we deny it or we throw it on the other person's heap for our spouse to clean up.

On your paper, write down the things you bring to the junk pile. Is it anger or sulkiness? Do you avoid problems rather than deal with them? Are you not around enough? List whatever problems you honestly think your spouse might say you bring to the marriage.

3. Envision success. This step requires that you envision what your marriage would be like without all of the problems. Envision happiness, togetherness, mutual support, and affection. As soon as you've envisioned success in your mind, move on to the final step of the Rectangle Solution.

4. Plan for success. With a vision of success firmly in mind, the next step is determining how to attain it. This means developing a strategy and fine-tuning your goals.

In the case of my fellow church member, the question was how to get his wife to stop being so argumentative and to start being more affectionate. The answer was to stop answering her taunts and arguments with his own barbs and to have the self-discipline it takes not to be baited into an argument.

Next, he had to decide what he was doing to cause her frustration. What part of the mess belonged to him? What was he doing to contribute to her quarrelsome and unaffectionate behavior? As it turned out, he found that the best way to find these things out was simply to ask her. Imagine that!

The next week, that same man stopped me after the church service with an update: "The minute I asked her those questions, she cried," he told me. "She said she had been trying to get me to see her side of our problems for years, and that she had given up. She even apologized for being so quarrelsome and she said we should consider getting into counseling. We had the best week together that we have had in months!"

The beauty of the Rectangle Solution is that it always leads you back to square one, as it did in my friend's marriage. When he gained a new perspective concerning his problems, he was able to see how he had contributed to the mess.

How about you? Are you trying to meet your spouse's needs, hoping that he or she will change, only to have your efforts rebuffed? Maybe it's time for you to gain a new perspective into your part in your marital problems!

CHAPTER NINE

Avoiding Potholes

Barry had grown so negative and pessimistic over his marriage that counseling almost seemed pointless. He was ready to give up on the whole thing.

While negativity and pessimism are sometimes understandable emotions, they are the "silent killers" in any relationship. Like an undetected cancer, they can slip into a marriage and surface when the relationship is in trouble.

For Barry, these two emotions served as a defense from the pain of an unhappy seven years of marriage. Together they kept him from being hurt by his wife again. If he ignored her when she failed to acknowledge an advance in his career, it was no big deal. If she put him down, he could deal with it. Since Barry anticipated the worst, a little more disappointment usually wasn't a huge problem for him.

In talking with Barry, I found a man who didn't think of himself as a negative person. He realized that he turned to this way of thinking only to distance himself emotionally from the misery of an unhappy marriage.

"You know, I never used to be negative," he said. "I was a positive person. I was always in a good mood. I looked forward to each new day. But now there's nothing to look forward to. Each day is just a reminder of how unhappy I was the day before. OK, so I'm negative. So what should I do, start acting more upbeat?"

"You're partially correct," I said. "But the cure for this particular problem has nothing to do with acting. You're not a phony. You're not an actor. You are not something you're not! The answer is about managing your expectations and being positive."

Since Barry lacked the confidence to communicate his needs and set boundaries, he had become increasingly frustrated, angry, and defensive toward his wife. He reacted to her nonverbal anger by creating even greater distance between them. As things stood at that time, any potential window of opportunity for change was boarded up and nailed shut.

Barry's attitude was a defense against his feelings of helplessness. He saw himself as passive, weak, and unable to assert his needs. When I informed him that he had the right to set boundaries and to communicate his needs to his wife, he looked at me as if I were speaking a foreign language.

Barry needed to imagine himself worthy of having feelings and an equal voice in his marriage. Once he accepted his position as an equal partner in the relationship, he was ready to move forward.

The same may be true for you. Like Barry, you may be either subconsciously or consciously putting up obstacles to marriage repair. The purpose of this chapter is to help you identify what obstacles you may need to tear down if you are going to get your marriage headed in the right direction.

ATTACK OF THE KILLER PRIDE

If there is anything that will keep you from successfully repairing your marriage, it is pride. Certainly, pride can damage a marriage. Pride is what causes spouses to blame each other for their problems. Pride can also keep them secluded from others for fear that people will see them for who they truly are. Pride keeps people from bringing their broken spirits and hurt feelings to God and others in humility, which is absolutely essential if there is to be healing.

Pride is evidence of a lack of maturity in relationships. It keeps us from having real empathy for a spouse who may be struggling emotionally, and it keeps us from making ourselves available to our spouses.

God's Word continually warns us against being prideful: "When pride comes, then comes disgrace, but with humility comes wisdom" (Prv 11:2). If you don't want to hamstring your marital repair efforts, get your priorities in order and rid yourself of pride!

No pain, no gain. Pain is a necessary byproduct of growth in your marriage and will most certainly be a part of repairing an unhappy relationship between husband and wife. How uncomfortable are you willing to become while repairing your marriage?

The difference between success and failure as you work to repair your marriage is in how you deal with emotional hurts that are sure to come. Just think of your pain as an emotional warning system that alerts you to problems within your relationship. Discover the origin of your pain and express it to your spouse, in love.

If the thought of emotional pain causes you to have second thoughts about going through the processes I've discussed, consider this story. A friend of mine was recently diagnosed with leukemia. After a full battery of tests was completed, her doctor explained her options for treatment. There were several treatments available, all following their own progression. None of the treatments sounded very pleasant, since they all had potentially significant side effects, some so distasteful and unpleasant that my friend was hesitant to begin the process at all!

But for those of us who loved and cared about this person, the decision was simple: Do whatever was *necessary* to get better! After a period of time to adjust to the news of her disease, my friend decided to begin treatment.

Your marriage restoration process will require you to make a similar commitment. Realize that you are considering this process because your marriage is sick. It may even be dying! Yes, the reparative process can be painful, but that pain is only temporary. divorce or emotional separation lasts a lifetime.

Reliving the past. As your past fades into memories, those memories hopefully become road maps to a better future. However, if you don't understand your past, your direction is blurred and you wander off course. If you don't take time to understand your past, you may be doomed to repeat your mistakes.

Paul instructs us that the past is relevant to us as a teacher: "These things happened to them as examples and were written down as warnings for us, on whom the fulfillment of the ages has come" (1 Cor 10:11).

By not using the past as a teacher, we're destined to repeat the same mistakes. For example, an adult whose father or mother was an alcoholic will often marry an alcoholic, presumably attempting to repair the lost relationship with his or her alcoholic parent.

Understand the hurts and losses of your past and then put them behind you. Work through emotional relics and resist the urge to dredge them up when things go wrong, only to repack them when the crisis ends.

Fear of being afraid. Fear can often immobilize people. But ask yourself, which is more frightening: remaining in a constant state of agitation, sadness, and anger over the condition of your marriage, or overcoming your anxieties and having faith that your efforts will change your marriage?

Don't be distracted or frightened by lingering questions as you strive to improve your marriage. It's normal to ask serious questions as you move forward in this area. Remember, you are dealing not just with your own thoughts and emotions but with those of another person.

As I've pointed out earlier, repairing a marriage isn't for the faint of heart. But don't let fear dash your chance for a better marriage.

False expectations. As you embark upon the all-important mission of repairing your marriage, remember not to get caught up in false expectations. Positive change requires time and attention, along with large portions of grace, truth, boundaries, support, and knowledge. It won't be easy, and it may take time.

After you've initiated positive changes in your relationship, don't expect your spouse to instantly become your "dream date." Give him or her time to recognize and adjust to this new standard of mature relating.

Another risky expectation is believing you have the power to *make* your spouse change. Rest assured, you can't force anybody to change. You can, however, change yourself. Your changes will influence and encourage your spouse to change.

Remember, there's no such thing as an "ideal" marriage. Let go of unreasonable expectations whenever possible. Resolve to change only what is changeable, while learning to understand and tolerate what is not.

What's yours is mine. Many marital problems involve one spouse taking responsibility for things that fall outside of his or her personal boundaries. This includes things such as feelings, attitudes, behaviors, values, time, energy, and love.

Such a mindset sabotages all the hard work you are trying to accomplish in your marriage. Until you work on establishing clear boundaries and taking responsibility for yourself, you will continue to experience disappointment and frustration in your marriage.

Keep reminding yourself that you can't force (manipulate) your spouse to do what he or she doesn't want to do or doesn't understand. Feel free to communicate your needs, but don't try to force someone to be something he or she is not.

Being a victim. As we've already learned, victims are chronic manipulators, blamers, defeatists, and complainers. They would rather rot in this negative mindset than communicate their needs directly and risk further pain.

But remember, you don't have to be a victim. You have the power to change your circumstances. If you catch yourself feeling helpless, remember that it's your right to make your needs known. Exercise that right in your marriage!

Misusing anger. In the hands of the wrong person—such as an immature spouse—anger can be a lethal emotion. It separates couples, blocks communication, seeks to dominate, and is vengeful.

For the mature spouse, however, anger can be a healthy emotion. It sounds a defensive alarm whenever our personal boundaries are threatened or violated. It also alerts us to problems within our marriage, which can then be directly and specifically addressed.

Anger is unavoidable, especially when marriages are going through tough times. But dealing with your anger on a mature level will speed up the restorative process in your marriage. When you're about to "lose it," ask yourself what you are really angry about. Very often, it won't be what originally made you angry. Try to isolate the root of your anger and address only that issue.

Apology neglected. Many of us find it easier to apologize to our boss, teachers, friends, relatives, and kids than we do to our spouse.

You're going to make mistakes as you apply your new knowledge. If you accidentally step on your spouse's feelings, apologize just as soon as you are aware of your error. Your ability to acknowledge your mistakes, apologize, and ask for forgiveness will make it easier for your mate to do the same.

The Bible goes to great lengths to point out the importance of forgiveness and repentance. I consider the words "I'm sorry" to be the gatekeeper of both. No question, you'll discover the connection between the grace and forgiveness you demonstrate and the grace and forgiveness you receive.

An eye for an eye. Skirmishing to see who can score the last punch produces no winners in a marriage relationship. Somebody must take the high ground and call a cease-fire.

But just because you've called a truce doesn't mean your spouse will recognize your efforts and stop fighting. Your spouse may fight purely out of habit. Or that person might think you're lulling him or her into a false sense of security while you regroup for another offensive. Instead of telling your spouse how' much you've changed, demonstrate it over a period of time.

Tell your spouse you've reached a decision: You don't want to argue, disagree, or fight as much as in the past. Don't make all of the friction look like your spouse's fault. Expect to be challenged at times. Meet those challenges with grace and forgiveness, and your spouse will soon see that you are truly intent on changing.

Bad timing. Timing is very important when it comes to working on your marriage. For example, do you select the right moment to bring up difficult subjects? Good marriages aren't based on "walking on eggshells," but you should try to gauge your spouse's mood before bringing up difficult issues in the marriage.

You probably already know the best times to approach your spouse. Bringing up your needs while your spouse is occupied with something, for example, isn't advisable or productive. Pick and choose your spots wisely and don't unload accrued anger all at once.

Guerrilla tactics. Some people have the tact and diplomacy of a military junta. They want results, and they'll stop at nothing to secure an unconditional surrender from their spouse. They may even try the hit-and-run tactics seen in what is known as guerrilla warfare.

There are several tactics you should avoid as you move into position to work on your marriage. They include guilt, shame, embarrassment, manipulation, and pressure.

Consider exchanging the weapons listed above for the following olive branches: tact, love, honesty, diplomacy, and patience.

The Bible is replete with stories and proverbs about the virtues of patience, but no story illustrates the promise of patience like the parable Jesus tells in Luke 13:6-9:

"A man had a fig tree, planted in his vineyard, and he went to look for fruit on it, but did not find any. So he said to the man who took care of the vineyard, 'For three years now I've been coming to look for fruit on this fig tree and haven't found any. Cut it down! Why should it use up the soil?'

"'Sir,' the man replied, 'leave it alone for one more year, and I'll dig around it and fertilize it. If it bears fruit next year, fine! If not, then cut it down.'"

The enemy of patience is instant gratification, wanting everything NOW! Try viewing the marriage restoration process as you might a remodeling job at your home. Restoring a kitchen, for example, requires the right tools, expertise, attention, and plenty of patience.

Those are twelve obstacles to be wary of as you restore your marriage. No doubt you will probably identify a few more obstacles of your own. Even if you erect a new barrier in your marriage, don't give up. Seek your spouse's forgiveness and start again.

And don't forget to pray. If possible, pray with a close friend or two on a daily basis for your goals.

Pray! Be positive! With God, all things are possible, including a happy marriage!

CHAPTER TEN

Married, but Sleeping Alone
(Sex, a Barometer to Intimacy)

Married couples usually aren't shy about discussing sex. The problem is that they just can't discuss it with one another! Why do husbands and wives have such a problem discussing this very important subject with each other?

Even when I bring up the topic of sex during marriage counseling, I often find myself looking back at two blushing faces. Obviously, many married couples are painfully uncomfortable talking about sex.

I recently met with a pair of newlyweds who were struggling in their sexual relationship. After a little ice-breaking conversation, I asked them about their premarital counseling at church, specifically what was said concerning sex.

"We met with the pastor several times," the husband said sheepishly. "He told us that intercourse was a loving act between a husband and his wife. That was about it."

I wasn't surprised to hear that the subject of sex was merely brushed over during this couple's premarital counseling. That is a story I've heard countless times as a counselor.

As squeamish as many of us are when it comes to sex, is it any wonder how many couples struggle with issues of sexual intimacy? Let's face it, parents don't say much to their kids about sex, except for DON'T! Dads tell their sons how to change the oil, spark plugs, and flat tires. They talk about how to earn a living and take care of money. More often than not, fathers talk to their sons about everything but sex.

And moms don't fare much better. They teach their daughters how to run a home and care for children. But they never seem to get around to talking about sex.

Considering the importance of a sexual relationship to a good marriage, this lack of preparation is very perplexing. Whatever the reason, too many husbands and wives are painfully insecure when it comes to talking about intimacy. Consequently, experimentation and open communication about what pleases us is left to chance.

When a marriage begins sliding into disrepair, a loss of sexual intimacy is usually the first symptom. Why? Because most women require emotional intimacy to feel good about having sex, while men only need the opportunity.

Since husbands and wives view sex so differently, it often becomes a totally separate marital issue. Sexuality is one of the main ways that men express their affection toward their mates. In fact, most men only feel emotionally attached when there is an adequate and satisfying sexual aspect to their marriage.

When men are rebuffed sexually, they become insecure about themselves and their marriages. Sexual frustration fuels their self-doubt. Many husbands start resenting their wives for what they see as a lack of love, care, and concern for their needs. They can begin to question the worth of a sexless relationship.

Right or wrong, men often view themselves as primary breadwinners in their families. In return, they expect a reasonable amount of sexual intimacy.

A wife—particularly one who works—might see that way of thinking as an unreasonable expectation. "I work full-time, too. I take care of the house, the kids, and the chores. And, come to think of it, I make nearly as much money. So what's the deal?"

The wife may have a point. But at the same time, she needs to realize that men view sexuality differently than women.

VERBALIZING AFFECTION

Most women are comfortable communicating their love through words and expressions of love, such as hugs, kisses, and cuddling. Women have a number of ways of sending and receiving loving signals. But men are usually less adept at communicating their love. They are generally less prone to tactile displays of affection. For some husbands, verbalizing love seems like speaking an unknown language.

Here's an illustration: On the eve of their twentieth wedding anniversary, a wife turns to her husband and asks, "Why don't you ever say 'I love you' anymore?"

"Look, dear," he replies, "I told you I loved you twenty years ago, and I'm still here. What more do you want?"

Intimacy issues are usually the result of unexpressed needs. For example, a wife needs her husband to verbalize his affection toward her. "If he cared," she reasons, "he'd know what to say."

You need to remember that no matter how much you have in common with your spouse, the two of you are completely different people. What may seem obvious to you is obscure to him, and vice versa.

SEXUALLY STUCK

As with any area of a happy marriage, a good sex life requires caring communication. Without it, you will have a situation like that of Ed and Beth.

"I didn't want to bring this up during our first session," Ed said at the beginning of marriage counseling. "But, I'm frustrated, sexually speaking."

As soon as Ed uttered the "S" word, his wife, Beth, rolled her eyes, slouched in her seat, crossed her legs, and folded her arms. If body language were audible, Ed would need earplugs.

"OK, I've been putting some pressure on her, but why not?" he said. "I work long hours and make a good living. I do my chores like a good little boy. I'm a great dad. I go to church almost every Sunday. All I ask is that she consider my needs. It's like sleeping alone every night."

Ed sounded more like a prosecuting attorney than a husband.

"She has a nice car, nice clothes, goes to the health club, lunches with her girlfriends, and runs up our credit card debt at the mall. She's a great mom, a good cook, and all that. But she makes me feel like an 'oversexed pervert' because I'd like to make love more than once a month! If it were up to her, we'd probably make love once a year... unless she had a headache that night."

He thinks she's undersexed and she thinks he's a sex addict. This is typical thinking between two people who have distanced themselves emotionally and physically.

"Anything else, Ed?" I asked.

"No," he said, softening his tone. "Isn't that enough? We'd have a good relationship if she enjoyed sex. Change that, and you're a miracle worker, doc!"

Meanwhile, Beth had practically disappeared beneath the cushions on my couch. Even after seven years of marriage, she was clearly uncomfortable when it came to talking about sex.

"What do you think of what Ed had to say, Beth?" I asked.

"I'm not sure what to say at this point," she said, glancing away. "He's probably right, I guess. Maybe I should have sex with him more often."

"There!" Ed interrupted. "That's exactly how she reacts when I get upset at home. She says yes as if it's a chore or something. Like doing the laundry or shoveling snow off the walk!"

"Go ahead, Beth," I urged. "There are always two sides in a troubled marriage."

Wiping away tears, she gathered the strength to finally verbalize her feelings.

"Do you really want the truth, Ed?" she said, looking straight at her husband. "The truth is you're lousy in bed. Your idea of making love is to 'knock it out' between dinner and giving the kids a bath. And I'm supposed to enjoy it?"

It was Ed's turn to sink into the cushions, as his wife unloaded years of pent-up feelings on the subject.

"I've tried to leave hints," she continued. "Remember that manual on the nightstand? Who do you think put it there? You say I don't enjoy sex. You're right. But have you ever wondered why? Could it be that you don't know that it takes more than two minutes to satisfy a woman sexually? I'm surprised you don't start the shower before we make love, so it's warm when you're done!

"After chasing our kids around all day, cleaning the house, cooking dinner, bathing them, and getting them ready for bed, there's still one major chore left: you! I can either avoid you sexually, and put up with your moping, or give in to something I really don't want at that moment.

"Look, you have a lot of good qualities, but you've never taken the time to learn what I need from you sexually. And that hurts. You say you feel alone in bed? Well, so do I. I'm sad to say I'd rather feel alone than have sex with you. Getting your jollies is all that matters to you."

This was obviously not an enjoyable session for Ed and Beth. They were both unloading years of a frustration that came from a lack of communication. But it was productive, because it was the start of their talking about something they had previously avoided addressing.

"THE TALK ..." BETTER LATE THAN NEVER

Sexual problems such as Ed and Beth's come about partly as a result of poor communication that starts in adolescence. Let's face it, we parents are notoriously poor at communicating with our children about sex.

Most parents approach "the talk" in one of three ways, two of which lead to sexual dysfunction in later life.

The first group (Christian parents are masters of this one) communicate to their kids that sex is sinful and dirty. In doing so, they send a powerful message that often carries into marriage.

A second group of parents avoid the subject altogether. "The less said, the better," they reason. "After all, our parents never talked to us about sex and we turned out fine." Unfortunately, their children often find it painfully difficult to express their sexual needs and desires in their adult lives.

The final group of parents—a small group, unfortunately—openly discuss sex with their children as a natural human feeling and emotion, a special declaration of love between two married people. People from these well-balanced homes generally have fewer problems involving sexual issues. From my observations, I would venture to say that the majority of married people grew up in families that fit with the first two groups.

To test that assumption, which I based on years of marriage counseling, I decided to conduct my own sex survey.

First, I devoted portions of several radio programs to the topic of sex and marriage. The switchboard immediately lit up as sixty-four callers managed to get through and take the "on-air" survey.

In order to make my survey somewhat more scientific, I also distributed the same survey to seven Christian marriage counselors and asked them to circulate it among their patients in therapy. Forty-nine surveys were returned from this group for a total of 113 responses.

The results of the survey were as follows. Answer each of the following questions as honestly as you can to see how you compare.

Question	Radio	Patient
1. Growing up, my parents talked:		
a. openly and honestly about sex	35%	8%
b. little or none about sex	44%	62%
c. mostly as if sex were a shameful subject	21%	30%
2. I received:		
a. a moderate amount of sexual instruction from my parents	60%	32%
b. considerable sexual instruction from my parents	21%	12%
c. almost no sexual instruction from my parents	19%	56%
3. I am ___ with my sexual relationship.		
a. very satisfied	62%	6%
b. fairly satisfied	22%	11%
c. not very satisfied	9%	47%
d. unsatisfied	7%	36%
4. When it comes to sex, I am		
a. shy	21%	41%
b. modest	32%	48%
c. open minded, adventuresome, and ready to experiment	47%	11%
5. Same question regarding my spouse:		
a. shy	20%	42%
b. modest	40%	51%
c. open minded, adventuresome, and ready to experiment	40%	7%

6. If I were to assign a letter grade to my spouse
   for his or her attentiveness to my sexual needs,
   I would grade him or her.

a. A	41%	4%
b. B	49%	8%
c. C	8%	33%
d. needs improvement	2%	55%

7. When it comes to our sex drives,

a. we are a good match	48%	12%
b. he wants sex more often	32%	58%
c. she wants sex more often	19%	9%
d. we're incompatible	1%	21%

SURVEY CONCLUSION

As you can see, there were significant differences between the two groups. My listeners represented a cross section of marriages, both good and bad, while the respondents from those in counseling were more typical of people already struggling in their relationships.

In general, my survey indicated the following conclusions:

1. Couples whose parents openly discussed sex when they were young tended to have happier sex lives in marriage.

2. Couples in marriage counseling routinely reported unhappy or less-than-satisfying sex lives.

3. Couples in marriage counseling rated their mates as average to needing improvement as sexual partners.

4. Husbands in marriage counseling usually regarded their wives as being less sexual than they would like.

5. Couples in marriage counseling tended to be more shy and less open about discussing sexual needs.

THE BOTTOM LINE

When a couple stops relating sexually, the relationship is usually struggling in other areas as well. On the other hand, show me a happy marriage, and I'll show you two people who are meeting each other's sexual needs. As a result, a couple's sex life can be an accurate barometer of the overall condition of their bond.

That's why it's important to continually monitor the intimacy in your relationship. For example, ask yourself if shyness, insecurity, embarrassment, or lack of sexual knowledge is contributing to your feelings of loneliness. If the answer is "yes" or "maybe," then it's time to consider some reparative steps.

WHERE DO I START?

If you are feeling alone in your relationship, you probably identified more closely with the survey responses from the marriage counseling group. Keep in mind, though, that even happily married couples go through seasons when sex is a source of frustration. It may be a major hurdle, such as Beth and Ed's situation, or a minor obstacle overcome through communication and a little extra effort.

Either way, assessing the state of your sex life should be your first step. With that in mind, take some time to fully answer the following questions. Your answers should provide insight into your own sexual relationship.

1. Are you sexually satisfied?
- If yes, then why? If no, then why not?
- If yes, when, why, and how?

2. Do you think your spouse is sexually satisfied?
- If you don't know, then why don't you know?
- Why haven't you asked?
- What would you do if you found out your spouse wasn't satisfied?

3. *Is sex something you look forward to?*
   - If so, then why? If not, then why not?
   - Does your spouse look forward to sex?
   - Have you ever asked him or her?
   - What would prevent you from asking now?

4. *Do you care more about your partner's sexual needs than your own?*
   - If you don't, why not?
   - Does your partner seem to care more for your needs than his or hers?
   - Have you ever asked your partner what he or she likes sexually? Why or why not?
   - Do you know what turns your spouse on as well as what turns him or her off? Why not ask?
   - What do you think would happen if you showed more interest in your spouse's sexual needs than your own?

5. *Do you enjoy having sex?*
   - If not, why not and what can you do to change this?
   - Are there physiological problems that prevent you from enjoying sex? If so, have you sought medical attention?
   - Is it that your spouse doesn't know how to please you?
   - Is it that your spouse doesn't care about pleasing you?
   - Have you asked for your needs to be met?
   - Is there anything else about your spouse and his or her sexuality that keeps you from enjoying sex? If there is, you owe it to yourselves to discuss it.

6. *Do you avoid sex?*
   - Why?
   - Are you angry or frustrated at your spouse for other issues and it's just showing up in this area?
   - What are the other issues that you're avoiding?
   - Do you think that withholding sex will get your spouse to try harder to please you in other areas?

7. *Do you want to talk about sexual wants and needs, but it's just too difficult?*
   - Why? Where did this start?
   - What are you afraid of if you were to begin talking about sexual needs?
   - Are you afraid of having to follow through?

8. *Do you feel sexually unattractive?*
   - What can you change and what can't you change to make yourself feel more attractive?
   - Are you being too harsh and critical of yourself?
   - Have you asked your spouse if he or she feels you are unattractive?

9. *Is your spouse sexually attractive to you?*
   - If not, what can he or she change and what can't he or she change?
   - Are you being too critical?
   - Have you asked him or her to change?
   - Are you making the mistake of comparing?

10. *Are you sleeping in separate rooms?*
    - If you are, why?
    - What is the message you are trying to communicate to your mate?
    - Why are the differences between you and your mate being avoided?

If you answered each question thoroughly and honestly, you probably have a better idea of what's right and what's wrong with your sex life. Your next move is to keep working through the questions until you have repaired those things that you are able to repair.

UNDERSTANDING YOUR DIFFERENCES

It would take a dozen books to chronicle the physical, mental, emotional, and sexual differences that God created between men and women.

Take sexual arousal, for instance. It's been said that for sex to happen, women need a reason and men just need a place. Men are visual creatures who often fall into the trap of comparing their wives to other women, sexually and otherwise.

Women, on the other hand, usually compare less visually and more emotionally. They identify a desirable attribute in a man such as sensitivity or sense of humor. Subconsciously, they may attempt to train their spouses to be more like the other man.

For husbands, sex takes place in the bedroom, but for wives, sex takes place nearly everywhere else, emotionally speaking. Husbands hear this: Tending to your wife's nonsexual, intimate needs will translate into sexual satisfaction! Anyone can be charming and attentive.

Showing your affection *outside the bedroom* means holding her hand in public, putting your arm around her at the movie, kissing her romantically and cuddling in bed without sexual gratification having to be a part of it. It means calling to ask her how her day is going and ending the conversation with "I love you." It means sending flowers for no particular reason or leaving her a card that simply says, "Hi, I love you." It means really listening, even when the subject doesn't interest you. It means putting down the newspaper and making eye contact when she speaks to you.

Some husbands take the position that they got married so they wouldn't have to do that stuff anymore. If married men would put half the time and effort into romancing their wives that they did during courtship, there would be a lot fewer sexually dysfunctional marriages around.

Be willing to consistently invest your time, effort, patience, attention, and love in your marriage. Over time, your efforts should reap healthy sexual dividends.

WHAT IS CLOSENESS?

Husbands and wives also evaluate physical and emotional closeness differently. For example, a man generally feels a sense of closeness when (a) sex is frequent and satisfying, (b) his wife keeps a tidy house, and (c) she feeds him.

In contrast, a woman feels closeness when (a) he demonstrates his affection outside the bedroom, (b) he is sensitive to her needs, and (c) he is a good father and provider.

The key to a happy and fulfilling marriage is to understand these basic differences and make adjustments whenever possible.

It is possible, for example, for men to adjust to be more communicative and romantic prior to making love. It is also possible for a woman to recognize that there are circumstances, such as time constraints, that don't allow for as much romancing as she would like.

In short, men are bottom-line oriented, while women measure intimacy through subjective feelings and emotions. Neither is wrong, just different. That's the way God made us. Troubles arise when we try to change our partners rather than attempting to adjust to one another's needs and limitations.

VISUAL INFIDELITY

Visually and variety-driven, men are often tempted by what they see—a shiny, new Corvette or an attractive receptionist at work. Some men learn the hard way that a new Corvette will destroy them financially, while the receptionist may destroy them emotionally, then financially. Thankfully, God gave men a sense of propriety to protect them from their visual temptations.

Unfortunately, that sense is dormant in many husbands, since statistics indicate 40 to 60 percent of all married men have had extramarital affairs. For married women, the numbers are 20 to 40 percent.

I've found that issues over intimacy often lead to infidelity for both husbands and wives. Here are a few key underlying reasons:

(a) A man's visual variety orientation and tendency to compare his wife to other women.

(b) A wife's belief that she can change her husband.

(c) A lack of understanding and control of these sexual urges (husband *and* wife).

(d) An inability to ask for those needs to be met within the marriage (husband *and* wife).

WITHHOLDING INTIMACY

Withholding intimacy—a popular and not-so-subtle form of manipulation—flourishes in marriages where neither party has learned how to resolve conflicts. Couples withhold intimacy when (a) they don't know how to state their needs directly or honestly, or (b) they have learned that the honest, direct route doesn't always have the desired effect.

Some women withhold sex from their husbands as a silent protest, a nonverbal way of saying, "No sex until you start meeting my emotional needs!" It's like a mother saying to her child, "No ice cream until you've finished your dinner." Most husbands, however, are reluctant to tackle any marital issues while a sexual schism exists, and this perpetuates a destructive cycle in the relationship.

BREAKING THE WITHHOLDING CYCLE

If you recognize that there is intimacy being withheld in your marriage, you need to take the lead in breaking this cycle. This may require things such as learning to be less inhibited or being more open to sexual exploration and experimentation.

For you wives, breaking the withholding cycle might mean initiating sex (if your husband usually assumes this role). You might also purchase a couple of negligees or take him to the intimate apparel section at your favorite department store so he can help you pick something out.

You might feel reluctant to have your husband pick something out because you're afraid he'll pick something you would be too self-conscious to wear. He might pick out something shocking, but remember, his choices speak volumes about his desires for you. Most men want a saint as a wife and mother, but something more exciting in the bedroom.

For you husbands: Your first step might be to use a little personal hygiene. Get rid of your five o'clock shadow, take a shower and do something about your breath. I'm not saying that you are necessarily a slob, but you need to treat these times with your wife as special. Make yourself as attractive as possible!

And you know how you like it when your wife wears something sexy to bed? Chances are, she'd like the same from you! Why not pick up something from the "jungle" collection at the mall? The surprise that you took the trouble to purchase something for her eyes only will pay dividends.

For both spouses: It also helps if you keep yourself from putting on too much excess weight. Not only will you look more appealing, you'll feel better and be healthier.

Finally, a trail of discarded clothing might look enticing in the movies. But chances are a wife won't appreciate it. Husbands, put your dirty socks in the laundry basket and hang up your pants. You'll be amazed how sexy some women find these simple acts.

You might also arrange to send the kids off to grandma's house, so the two of you can be alone. You could try a hot tub or a hot bubble bath as alternatives to the bedroom, or you could spend the night in a local hotel. Feel free to let yourself go. You're married, you have that privilege!

SHARING YOUR SECRETS

It's amazing how many couples have vivid sexual imaginations, yet never share their creativity—at least not with their spouses. Instead, too many couples limp along with a dull, unfulfilling sex life, rather than risk divulging their sexy secrets.

Here is what I hope can be a painless way of breaking the ice:

First, get a clinical (not pornographic) book of sexual positions and techniques. You can find these books at many bookstores. Next, select two highlighting markers, one color for each of you. As you leaf through the book, highlight any sexual positions or techniques that appeal to you. Your spouse will follow you, doing the same. When you are both finished, discuss what each of you has highlighted. You can then begin experimentation.

One important note: Don't feel compelled to try everything your spouse highlights and don't insist on trying something your spouse objects to. If you are uncomfortable with a given selection, suggest an alternative. Above all, if you have agreed to try one or more of your mate's highlighted selections, follow through. Failing to do so will heighten his or her expectation that nothing is ever going to change in your sex life.

If the use of a book doesn't interest you, you can try three-by-five cards. Simply write down a few of your sexual desires, one per card. Next, set a date and exchange cards. Do whatever your spouse has written on the card. Again, don't automatically refuse, or we are back to square one.

THE WINDOW OF OPPORTUNITY FOR INTIMACY

When a couple's libidos (sex drives) differ, I often suggest setting aside one or two nights a week for sexual intimacy. I suggest selecting which nights they will be ahead of time. This serves several purposes: First, it takes the pressure off the wife, who may feel pressured for sex. It also enables healthy sexual tension to build, making those two nights highlights of the week. Couples should view those nonsexual days as a window of opportunity to be physically close to their mates without every caress having to lead to sex.

In some marriages, sex is virtually nonexistent. These couples sometimes face the added pressure of "first time" anxiety that prevents them from being sexual. In these cases I recommend a four-week warm-up to sex:

First week: The couple will lie in bed together and talk only. No physical contact during the first week.

Second week: They only hold hands while lying in bed talking. Again, no sex is recommended in this week.

Third week: Both husband and wife may touch or stroke each other in nonsexual places as they lie in bed. He might rub her neck and shoulders, and she might give him a back massage. Again, refrain from sexual contact.

Fourth week: Sexual touching may begin. If intimacy is mutually agreed upon at this point, have fun!

This system is usually successful in reinitiating sexual intimacy in a marriage. By the way, this was the method that helped Beth and Ed rekindle their flagging love life.

Above all, don't be selfish sexually. Your number-one objective should always be to meet the intimacy needs of your spouse. Of course, that should be your mate's sole objective as well. That is the bedrock of a satisfying sex life in any marriage.

The Most Frequently Asked Questions in Marriage Counseling

I'm confident that many of you have already found at least some of the answers you've been searching for within this book. There are, however, a number of common questions that come up regularly in marriage counseling. The following "Q & A" is a list of the most frequent questions asked of me during counseling.

Q: How quickly can I expect to see results?
A: Dr. Paul Meier, a friend and cofounder of the Minirth-Meier Clinic, revealed a secret for weight loss that applies to many areas of our lives where expectations play a part. He said that one of the major reasons why so many people fail in their weight-loss goals is that they expect to lose too much weight too fast. His rationale is sound: "These people didn't gain the weight in ninety days, why should they expect to take it off that quickly?" He recommends trying to lose a few pounds a month, at approximately the same rate the weight was gained.

This book is designed to bring about results. How fast? That's influenced by several factors, including:

- *Length of marriage.* The longer the marriage has been in trouble, the longer the restoration process is likely to take.
- *Your ability to minimize setbacks.* When minor or major setbacks occur, the speed with which you recover and get back on track will influence the restoration process.
- *Your resolve and the consistency of your efforts.*
- *Your spouse's willingness to change.*
- *Your willingness to change.*
- *Your ability to understand and apply what you've learned.*

Q: What if I don't see the changes I anticipated?
A: Be sure your expectations are realistic and attainable. And be patient. Being overly critical or anxious will hamper the overall process.

Q: Is a trial separation ever a viable option?
A: Separating is too easy and can become too comfortable. Most of us already know we can live by ourselves. The goal is to learn to live happily together, not apart. I've seen too many couples fail in their attempt to restore their marriage, due to a counselor's suggestion of a trial separation.

I only recommend a trial separation when one or both spouses are physically abusive. During these times, a short separation might be in order as both people cool off.

Q: Will change be constant or should I expect setbacks?
A: Improvements in your marriage will come in plateaus. You will probably see rapid improvement, followed by periods of little or no progress. You may even see a slight remission of progress. This is normal, so don't be alarmed.

When improvement is clear, acknowledge these advances. When improvement is slow or non-existent, you may bring it to your spouse's attention without being critical. Simply make an observation and invite dialogue to take the progress to the next plateau.

Q: How will I know if I need more help?

A: Restoring a marriage is a complex process. We all have varying degrees of aptitude. There may be situations where you'll need outside professional help. If so, don't feel like you've blown it. It's often the wise person who admits that it is time for a specialist.

Key indicators that signal the need for professional help include:

- An inability to recognize your part in the marital problems.
- The restoration isn't bringing about the desired results, despite your best efforts over a reasonable period of time.
- Your spouse is totally resistant to your efforts.
- You're too angry and resentful to focus your attention on further efforts.
- Your spouse is abusive.

Q: Should I tell my spouse about the book and my efforts?

A: Yes and no. If you believe your spouse will be receptive to your efforts, then by all means, tell him or her. On the other hand, if you have serious doubts about how the news will be received, then you are better off keeping silent.

I like the way Proverbs 29:11 (Living Bible) puts it: "A fool uttereth all his mind."

Q: How long should I wait before seeking help?

A: In the past, a rule of thumb has been to give the process six months of intensive effort before considering outside assistance. That doesn't mean, however, you shouldn't seek counseling earlier if both you and your spouse agree that it would be beneficial. Remember, the goal is to restore the marriage. If after six months of sincere effort you fail to see tangible improvements, you should explore additional assistance.

Q: What types of help are available?

A: In most metropolitan areas, finding good marriage help is relatively easy. Here are some resources to consider:

- Pastoral counseling (pastor, priest or lay pastor).
- Marriage counseling with a Christian professional.
- Marriage retreats sponsored by a church and taught by qualified professionals.
- Marriage classes or groups sponsored by a church.

Q: Are pastors a good place to start for help?
A: Pastors are generally a good resource for either providing marriage counseling or helping you secure further assistance.

Here are a few questions that you might ask your pastor prior to making your decision about counseling:

1. *How many couples has he helped through similar problems?*

2. *Does he or she acknowledge that marital problems can be symptoms of deep-rooted emotional issues, or does he or she imply that marriage problems are just symptoms of unconfessed sin?*

3. *Does he or she believe that the wife's job is simply to submit to her husband, no matter what the situation may be?*

4. *What is his or her plan for helping your marriage?*

5. *How many counseling sessions can he or she schedule to work with you?*

Q: What about Christian counseling versus secular counseling?
A: There are financial and geographical factors that may limit your ability to seek the specific type of counseling you want. When given the option, I would suggest that you seek a Christian marriage counselor.

It should also be noted that many secular counseling centers employ Christian counselors who simply don't advertise their faith.

Q: How do I know if he's really a Christian counselor?
A: Anyone can call themselves Christian counselors. Simply having a Bible on the shelf doesn't mean the counselor is qualified. Be a wise consumer. Here are a few things to ask:

1. *Will prayer be included in the counseling session?*

2. *Will you explain the Bible's viewpoint concerning divorce?*

3. *Do you ever counsel couples to separate or divorce?*

4. *What school did you attend and which licenses do you hold? (Look for accredited schools and counselors who hold current registrations or licenses in your state.)*

5. *How long have you been providing marriage counseling? (Five years or more of experience is preferable.)*

6. *Are you married? If so, how long? (Look for counselors who have been married more than ten years and have never been divorced. A divorce doesn't necessarily rule a person out, but it is a warning sign.)*

7. *How would you envision helping my marriage? What's your plan?*

8. *How long do you feel the counseling process will take? (Once a week for approximately six months is a reasonable length of time.)*

Q: How do I know if I've got a bad counselor?
A: Inadequate marriage counselors can be tough to spot early on. Your best bet is to go with your instincts after you've checked them out thoroughly. Some warning signs, however, include the following:

1. *Counsels out of his or her home.*

2. *Loses his or her temper.*

3. *Doesn't listen well or continually interrupts.*

4. *Only listens, offering very little interaction.*

5. *Doesn't assign homework.*

6. *Seems to favor or take sides.*

7. *Won't confront obvious problems.*

8. *After two or three sessions, you've learned little or nothing.*

9. *Seems intimidated by either you or your spouse.*

Q: How important is ongoing accountability?
A: Ongoing accountability is critical to the restoration of a marriage. Each spouse should be actively involved in his or her own weekly accountability, over and above the regular couple's counseling sessions. If you attend marriage counseling alone, consider finding a mentor—ideally, someone who can meet with you informally once a week. These meetings should allow for a free exchange of ideas. Your mentor is not intended to be another counselor, but a person encouraging you to succeed in your marriage. A mentor should be a mature Christian who has a solid marriage, a person you can call between sessions when things get difficult and a person who will reinforce your commitment and offer words of encouragement.

Q: How will I know if it is time to leave my marriage?
A: My suggestion is not to consider divorce as an option *unless you are in physical danger.* Having divorce in the back of your mind may hamper your efforts in restoring your marriage. Divorce should be excluded as a topic of conversation until after you've exhausted all available options (books, individual and couple's counseling, mentoring, and a reasonable period of time).

If your marriage shows no signs of improvement after all of your efforts, then it may be time to ask about your mate's intentions. Is divorce his or her ultimate goal? The human condition usually dictates that we're reluctant to make changes until our backs are against the wall. Be cautious, however, not to use this tactic at any point until you have exhausted all other available means of getting your mate's attention.

Q: How can Christians benefit from counseling?
A: Sadly, many Christians view professional therapy as a sign of spiritual weakness. That goes for self-help books, too. For some, buying a book entitled *Is Your Marriage on the Rocks?* would be as shameful as ducking into the "adult" section of the video store for a peek, then leaving with the latest Disney release.

Unfortunately, many churches aren't helping matters. Parishioners are often told that all of their problems can be solved through Scripture, a notion that contradicts the very essence of Christ. No doubt, our Lord could have waved his hand and solved all of man's ills for eternity. Instead, he enlisted the help of twelve others to spread the gospel, clearly suggesting a desire that people should help people.

The Bible does not advocate hiding from or avoiding our problems. We're told to seek the counsel of the Lord and be open to the wisdom of fellow Christians in times of need.

SUMMARY

Congratulations! The fact that you've read this entire book means your priorities are in order. It means you are ready to take action. Anyone can complain about their lives, but not everyone takes the initiative to make things better.

Unless I miss my guess, you've already incorporated some of the techniques from this book in your marriage. If not, I encourage you to begin right away. And don't forget the power of prayer throughout the reparative process. Pray often for God's will in your marriage. Keep in mind that he probably wants your marriage to work even more than we do.

I welcome your letters and comments. I can be reached by writing to:

Dr. Greg Cynaumon
c/o KBRT - AM 740
3183 Airway Avenue, Suite D
Costa Mesa, CA 92626
or
Dr. Greg Cynaumon
Minirth-Meier Clinic West
1028 Town & Country Road
Orange, CA 92668

Throughout Southern California, Dr. Cynaumon is heard from 3:00 P.M. to 6:00 P.M., Monday through Friday, on radio station KBRT, AM 740.